Letters from Lavender Cottage

Hastings in WWII and Austerity

A biography
by Victoria Seymour

First published in 2002
By Victoria Seymour

Copyright Victoria Seymour.

Email: mail@victoriaseymour.com
Website: www.hastings.uk.net

ISBN: 0-9543901-0-5

Printed in Great Britain by

impression IT.
26, Brunel Road
St Leonards on Sea,
East Sussex
TN38 9RT

I dedicate this book to the memory of John, my husband.

I extend my sincere thanks to Wendy Johnson of Canada for allowing me to use her family correspondence for "Letters From Lavender Cottage" and for her unfailing support and that of her family. I offer my gratitude to my own family for their encouragement, patience and technical advice during the preparation of this book. I wish also to recognise the help I have received from Hastings Reference Library staff, Bexhill Museum and local writers, historians and innumerable and unknown webmasters. Acknowledgements are due to The Hastings and St Leonards Observer for use of their archive material and to the many publishers of the book, The Chronicle of the 20th Century.

Dear Angelique,

Most people have a morning routine; since my computer became an important part of my retirement, mine includes getting connected to the Internet at once and looking at my email and web site messages.

On April 15th 2001, I found this message on the www.hastings.uk.net notice board:-

"Does anyone know if the house, Lavender Cottage, The Ridge, Hastings, is still there? A cousin of mine lived there for years. I believe she died in 1955. We have many letters written to my aunt, who sent her parcels during WW II and after, when supplies were short. They are an interesting account of that period of history."
Wendy Johnson from Canada

I emailed Wendy, confirming that the house still exists; the location is quite close to my village. I later emailed her a photo of the cottage, asking if it would be possible to see the letters. Wendy copied all of the nearly 100 letters and sent them to me. As I read them I became drawn into the accounts of the daily doings of their writer, Miss Emilie Crane and her house companions and longed to share the pleasure of the letters with others. I began an email correspondence with Wendy in Canada, which, incidentally, has become as interesting as the letters from the 1940s and 1950s.
I think that you will become as fond of Emilie as I have. Although she was a stranger to me, when I started to read the letters I felt as if I had actually met her and that her letters could be the foundation of a book.

My parents, who were a cook and gardener in Chislehurst in Kent, frequently had employers like Miss Crane. Before I was old enough for school and during the holidays, there was often no one to look after me at home when my parents were at work, so I had to go to the employer's house and make myself scarce, somewhere in the kitchen, garden or outbuildings. Sometimes, I met the mistresses of the houses; for the most part these women had been raised in comfortable circumstances, were kindly and properly educated and did, 'good works' for their church, local societies and impoverished families. They did not waste time on being fashionable. They wore a comfortable ensemble of sensible shoes and stockings, felt hats and tweedy, woolly garments. They had simple, 'bun' hair styles and good,

English complexions. They had a jaunty humour and a lively sense of duty; Emilie was probably a perfect example of this breed.

Emilie's letters of thanks, for food parcels, sent from Canada by her cousin Marion and her friend Beatrice, are a cheerful and vivid account of coping with the restrictions of war and post war austerity and the trials of the advancing years of herself and her two house companions, her life-long friend Miss Clare Marriott and their mutual friend, Mrs Edith Lake. I hope you enjoy your meeting with Emilie and find her life and character as heart-warming, funny and inspiring as I have.
Love from Victoria

Footnote: Angelique is my 25 year-old daughter-in-law. She was born and brought up overseas and came to the UK at the age of sixteen. The only personal anecdotes she has heard about WWII were those from her Dutch and Belgian grandparents.

Angelique and I share an enjoyment of reading and I knew she would be the perfect person with whom to share Emilie's letters.

1942

Lavender Cottage,
The Ridge,
Hastings,
East Sussex
June 9th 1942.

My Dear Marion,

I can't tell you how delighted I was to receive your lovely parcel this morning; it was a welcome surprise and more than kind of you to send it. I don't know how you came to choose the things most needed and such acceptable items. I think the things we have most missed here are butter and fruit; all the fats are so scarce and the rations do not allow us much, so we shall revel in nice bread and butter. As for oranges, the small consignment sent over is reserved for children under six, which is as it should be, therefore, we shall rejoice in the fruit juice.

The tea will be a treat; I gave my ration coupons to Miss Marriott, who can only drink china tea. A friend had some Orange Pekoe (tea) sent from British Columbia and I have been envying her so now it is my turn to smile! I am very intrigued with the egg powder and shall try it at the first opportunity. I have scoured Hastings for a saucepan cleaner, how did you think of that? Soap and sugar are of course rationed strictly. I can get saccharine but I do not care much for it; such sickly stuff. The serviettes will be very useful as the paper shortage is acute. Hence the notepaper I am using, taken from some old volumes, from a period when they used better paper than they do now. My best thanks for everything and the kind thoughts that came with them.

I do hope the above remarks do not sound as if we are in a bad way; it is only that things are in short supply. Lord Woolton has done very well; we all think that food distribution is better than in the Great War. We do miss some things, naturally, but we expect that in a terrible war. I think the light is beginning to come through at last, don't you? Hitler is not having a very pleasant time. All day the fighters and bombers go over us on their way to France and Germany. They are Canadians, Americans, British, Polish, French etc; we know they do some damage. We have had two raids recently, they were not nice and there were a good many casualties. My other friend's sister is an ambulance driver and she tells us some sad stories but everyone here is wonderfully cheerful and none doubt of ultimate victory. We had an exciting time last week when the wounded from the Commando raid on France were brought to the hospital here; I am sorry to say that one died.

I wish I could do more to help but one's age is against it. I took the first aid course and went to help in a First Aid Post but it was so damp I got pleurisy after three months and the doctor would not let me go there again. So I went for an anti-gas course and received a certificate but fortunately the Germans have not resorted to gas. I offered myself for clerical work but they wanted younger people, so I fell back on door-to-door collecting for the National Savings Campaign and that has been successful. (Emilie is 71 years old at his time) One can do knitting of course, but it isn't exciting to knit all the time; some of my pullovers would fit a large-sized giant! The garden is a great joy and we really have done well with vegetables but fruit is very shy and does not like The Ridge climate.

Well my dears I hope you will forgive this rambling on, there is little news to give you and each day is the repetition of another; planes overhead, air raid alerts and wireless news. By the way, I have not mentioned my family. They are all well except my sister-in-law who is now in a nursing home. Her mind has gone but she is happy and knows little of the war, which is a mercy, poor thing. I believe my nephew is well and he looks after his mother. Please give my love to everyone and much to yourself, with renewed thanks,
Yours affectionately Emilie.
P.S. this letter is a scrawl but the paper is not easy to write on

1942

Dear Angelique,

This is the first of only two letters written by Emilie during the WWII period. Here, she reveals her determination to do her duty in spite of her age and not very good health. With typical understatement she refers to the Hastings daylight raids as "not very nice", when, in fact, there was considerable loss of life, many casualties and the destruction of scores of buildings in the town. Hastings was in the front line when it came to air raids and in 1942 the town was the victim of low-level, tip and run raids, which happened without warning and left residents in a constant state of fear. There were thousands of Canadian soldiers billeted in the south east of England during the war and hundreds in Hastings; many lost their lives in a seafront bombing raid in May 1943.

It may be that the Canadians in the Hastings hospital Emilie mentions in this letter were carrying out a reconnoitre raid on the French coast, in preparation for the following August's commando raid, "Operation Jubilee", in which over nine hundred Canadians were killed or died of their wounds. Former WWII Irish Guardsman and Battle and Hastings resident, Ivor White, told me this story about the Canadians he met when he was a teenager:

"I applied to join the Home Guard and, lying about my age, I nervously attended an enrolment meeting at the local British Legion Headquarters. I hoped that they would not ask any awkward questions about my age because I had only just left school. However, I was duly enrolled on 29th January 1942 as a Home Guardsman and eventually issued with a uniform, a rifle, and ten rounds of ammunition.

I met lots of the Canadians billeted in Battle, those smartly dressed soldiers, with their charming manners, funny American-like accents, plenty of chocolate bars and large packets of "Sweet Caporal" cigarettes. No wonder the locals took them to their hearts. I quickly made friends with the team of Canadian Army motor mechanics known as the L.A.D, who had taken over the Maidstone and District Bus Garage at the bottom of Lower Lake, Battle. It was here that I helped to waterproof Jeeps and 15cwt trucks for the ill-fated 19th August dawn attack on Dieppe, in Northern France. Some failed to return; we

5

did not know that might happen at the time so I was not able to say a proper goodbye. One name stands out among the many, most of whom we only knew by their first name. "Hank" was a super guy from Ontario, and when I visit the war cemeteries of Northern France, as I often do, I'm glad I never knew his last name".

Housewives continued to cope with food struggles on the home front with recipe advice from the government. Lord Woolton was the Minister of Food and remembered for his wartime, economy recipe for Woolton Pie, a concoction of pastry and vegetables. Today's vegetarians would probably love it but it did not go down too well in the Britain of the 1940s, with its predominantly meat-eating population. About this time, my mother invented some potato cakes, flavoured with lots of onion and a scrap of our cheese ration. She put them on the table saying, 'Try it!' This tasty, experimental dish was named "tryits" thereafter.

I wonder if Emilie's remark, 'I scoured Hastings for a saucepan cleaner' was an intentional pun; it was one I think she would have enjoyed don't you? Emilie refers to the paper shortage; this of course extended to lack of paper for personal hygiene and I can tell you very few newspapers were put in the dustbin in wartime!

It was not only the household at Lavender Cottage that was pre-occupied with food; frequent announcements and opinions on the matter appeared in the local paper, The Hastings and St Leonards Observer. In the week of 13th June 1942 residents were informed in its columns that, "The new issue of ration books would take about two to three weeks and the Ministry of Food said it strongly disapproved of shopkeepers who tried to get new registrations from customers by unfair methods or who convey the suggestion that one retailer can offer greater security than another in the supply of rationed foods".

In the same edition we are reminded that war is not all action when we read that three WAAF Hastings girls, Aircraft Women Haste, Hills and Munday, are appealing for a gramophone, adding, "It is a good life we are leading but it gets a bit monotonous". In June 1942, Double British Summer Time was in effect, evenings were very long, with blackout time not starting till after 11:00pm. In May 1942, the British

1942

Government postponed its plans for fuel rationing after widespread opposition but there were some chilly lower limbs as the patriotic "bare legs for fashion", began to take on; I cannot see Emilie and her friends subscribing to this daring contribution to victory! James, the Lavender Cottage cat who we meet later, would probably not have liked the innovation of the Consultant Superintendent of The Peoples' Dispensary for Sick Animals, C H Gaunt. He published instructions on how to make a gas-proof cat and dog box, in which the pet should be encouraged to sleep habitually, in preparation for the worst.

In 1942 my father was aged 42 and suffering from a hernia and high blood pressure. He was considered unfit for military service but joined the Home Guard. He and his fellow "soldiers" used to go on training exercises and manoeuvres on the local commons and in the woods; his yarns of their exploits were not all that far removed from scenes in the TV sitcom, "Dad's Army." The extended, evening light enabled him to work at his gardening jobs until very late. Stuart Hibbard, the BBC announcer and newsreader, lived in Chislehurst and he was one of my father's employers. He rode round the village on a rusty old bicycle that was very out of keeping with his dignified, on-air manner.
Love from Victoria

1943

Lavender Cottage.   December 18th 1943.

(The envelope for this letter had a sticker on it marked, "opened by examiner 7336")

Dear Marion,

You can't imagine what a delightful surprise I had this morning. I happened to have got up at five because Miss Marriott (whom you may remember) was not at all well and I wanted to get her some tea and a hot water bottle. After breakfast, as it was so early, I did some washing, by 8.30 I felt very washed out. Then the postman came and handed me your parcel. I forgot all about being tired in my eagerness to open it. It was a joy!

I marvelled especially at the way you had remembered the little things that one cannot get here; you will know those to which I refer even though even though I don't mention them, though I am sure the censor would not object. My two friends gazed longingly at the cake, not having seen such for many months, but I was quite firm and said, "Not until Christmas Day, and if we can wheedle the butcher into giving us some suet and save the fat from our weekly rations, we can have a real Christmas Pudding with the raisins." I had much bother in preventing them from eating the latter. I can understand it, as dried fruit is most hard to get, except from the black market. I liked too, the little Christmas adornments on the parcels.

We have asked two invalid friends for Christmas Day and shall be able to give them a very nice dinner, thanks to you. The butcher promises mutton, he suggested pork but that is not suitable for invalids. Poultry is out of the question; I heard turkeys are selling at £5 each and chickens at 30 shillings or two pounds. It is outrageous but they say they can't get the feed for the birds. Of course the troops get the best food, which is as it should be.

We are fortunate in having the garden, as vegetables are such a good standby. I only wish I had tried the sweet corn this year but it was hardly the summer for it. I grew some two years ago and it did well, until it came to cooking it. I boiled it for four hours and it was like bullets!

We have had quite a peaceful time here of late with only occasional dives for the shelter and we hope this will last until Christmas is over at any rate. Things look hopeful don't they? But we try not to be over-optimistic, in accordance with Churchill's instructions. We have just heard he is a trifle better and we are very thankful. Will you kindly give my love to your mother and thank her for her card? It was good of her to remember. My very best thanks again for the lovely parcel and with love and every good wish to you.

Yours affectionately, Emilie.

Dear Angelique,

You will probably notice that Emilie does not mention the terrible air raids that Hastings suffered in 1943. She lived well outside the town, records show that only two high explosive bombs fell on The Ridge area during the entire war but I think her enquiring mind would have kept her up to date with local news. Maybe she did not want to refer to the terrible, local tragedies and that is why her letters recount, for the most part, domestic affairs. Perhaps she kept her comments to those of a more general nature, being conscious of the censor. I love Emilie's comment 'I boiled the sweet corn for four hours and it was still like bullets'. Cooks of her generation had probably never encountered this food before so it was natural that she resorted to the time-honoured British treatment for vegetables, boiling them into submission!

Emilie was writing as Hastings prepared for its fourth wartime Christmas, residents were asked to stay at home to help the war effort. Those who were lonely at Christmas could find "warmth and comfort with the Christian Alliance for Women and Girls", who were offering hospitality at 15, Cross Street St Leonards, from 25th-27th December for 1/- per day. I think this invitation would be more carefully worded these days! The efforts of Emilie and her counterparts as National Savings collectors must have paid off; Hastings' total savings for week December 11th 1943 was an astounding £8, 147. In the light of this figure, and added to Hastings' poverty and wartime shortages, the Christmas warning in the local paper, by Sir Harold McIntosh of the National Savings Committee to,' beware the Squander Bug, Hitler's secret weapon', sounds rather ironic.

Plummer Roddis, now Debenhams, the town centre department store, was refused a request put to the Hastings Food Control Committee, (very Orwellian) to open their restaurant. Councillor S. Riddle said that other nearby catering facilities must be taken into consideration. He also warned that, "Restaurants were filled with local people who were living in a parasitic way, instead of from their own rations". This extract, from the local paper, dated 18th December1943, goes some way to convey not only the severe shortage of food but also the stringent controls, by a battalion of wartime government departments, which were imposed on the people of Britain.

It would seem that the gramophone was often seen as a comfort for loneliness; General R. W. Stamp of Hastings made a newspaper request for a gramophone for the men on an isolated army camp site, 'for dancing and to pass the long winter evenings. Although Emilie does not make many references to national and international news in her letters, her mention of Churchill's health is telling. During the war he was a great, public morale booster and it is no surprise that Emile should comment on his well being. During December the government announced that there were only enough turkeys for one family in ten to have one so this was probably the contributing factor to the high price to which Emilie refers.

We had a very miserable winter in Chislehurst in 1943, not just from the cold and shortage of food and heating but because my brother Ron, who was 16, was seriously ill. He was admitted to Farnborough hospital with meningitis, his life was saved by penicillin, only for him to immediately develop a polio-type illness, which partially paralysed him and affected his speech. The air raids were particularly heavy; it was terrifying for him, already weakened by a long illness, to lie helplessly in hospital as bombs exploded all around.

Our cousins from Canada, Albert and Robert Burkin, who were in the Canadian army, arrived in Chislehurst and were billeted very near us; we saw a great deal of them. They seemed so healthy, strong and well fed in comparison with ourselves but every time they came to the house they brought supplies; tinned meat and fruit, cheese and butter, chocolates and sweets. We too had reason to be grateful to Canada.

I was later sent to stay with my mother's life-long friend in Glastonbury, Somerset. My mother needed a rest, she was worn out with the stresses of my brother's illness, the anxieties for her other son, who was in the Royal Navy in submarines and the punishing round of night-time raids. I felt desperately lonely in Somerset. I was not exactly an evacuee; there were no other "Lunnon", (as they said), children there, so I was something of an oddity and therefore an object of ridicule. I made the best of it, as children do, but it was a joyful day for me when, after ten months, I went home.

This seems a good time to mention the general effect of WWII on the British children, who are elderly people now. Many of us tend to be economical with everything; we save scraps of paper to serve as note-pads, use bars of soap down to the merest sliver and concoct meals from hoarded leftovers. We are the complete recyclers, very modern! More profound than this is the long term effects of living in constant fear of injury or death; we seem to be slightly anxious people but the upside is we are tremendous survivors!
Love from Victoria.

1946

Lavender Cottage.   March 16th 1946.

Dear Marion,

Your delightful parcel dated the 15th February came this morning and I really don't know how to thank you for it. Every thing is nice and will be a great treat. We couldn't resist cutting a slice off the cake but we did divide it into three pieces as it seemed much too soon to begin on it. However, they insisted on a taste; now fruit of all kinds is so scarce all cakes must be severely plain so you can guess how the sight of this one fascinated us. You do hit on the most needed things.

The ham is most acceptable. You see, we are given 1/3d (7p) worth of meat each per week and as the butcher includes a fine percentage of bone, it needs all the genius of my friend, who does the cooking, to make it last three days. Dried Eggs have been cut since the beginning of February, the supply of fresh ones is exceedingly erratic; sometimes three a week, sometimes none. Sugar is static at half a pound per week each unless you want jam or marmalade; in which case you can't have sugar. The cheese ration at 2 ounces per week does not offer much scope so you can be sure we are going to enjoy ourselves with your lovely present. I love the scourers; the last one you sent was good for six months. I wanted to try the noodles today but Miss Marriott said that was wasteful as the butcher came. I shall try the tea tomorrow; it looks so good.

I must apologise for not having replied to your letter earlier. The reason is that all three of us were seized with influenza, which has been rampant over here and one or the other of us was in bed for over a month, which made a fair amount of work and I could get no letters written, I was sorry to hear about your mother having bronchitis and hope she has made a good recovery. I don't know what kind of weather you are having but a bitterly cold winter is not good for chest complaints. We are somewhat outraged by the continual frosts and east winds, not to speak of sleet and fog in addition; it doesn't seem natural in England. The farmers are two months behind sowing the wheat and if the summer is short, well, I expect we will look to Canada as usual for our bread supply. She is always kind. The minister of food has mentioned rationing for bread too. I hope it won't come, if it does I will be summoned for feeding the birds!

You asked about The Ridge, yes it is on a height, of 500 feet above sea level. It runs up from the town and enjoys the coldest weather. But to compensate it is cooler than the seafront in summer. We are about 4 miles from Hastings proper and the country around is very pleasant but I hear rumours of a factory being built just across the road.

This seems a somewhat scrappy epistle, my excuse is that they have just put on the wireless and some horrible person is crooning, not that anyone likes crooning but the wireless was put on to hear 'The Week in Westminster' and everyone is too lazy or occupied to turn it off. Will you kindly give my love to your mother and I hope she is really strong again. I can never forget Cousin Emily, who learned to drive a car at 70, wasn't it? But I don't think that your mother is as strong as that. Thank you again for all your kindness, it was good of you. My love to you,
Affectionately, Emilie

1946

Dear Angelique,

Isn't it frustrating that there are only two letters from Emilie that give us some idea of her Hastings' life in wartime? But I expect things went on much the same as usual, as she herself would say. We do not know if letters were not written or if any written were lost. Do you remember that Wendy Johnson from Canada told us, on her visit to Hastings in March 2002, that she had conducted a very thorough search of the effects, after the death of her aunt, Marion Ellis, to whom the letters were written? We must presume there were none, as Marion saved everything.

Although this 1946 letter is written in peacetime, life was very far from returning to pre-war conditions, where food and other necessities are concerned. The holiday visitors to Hastings, beginning to trickle back, were told that they could demand three good meals a day on presenting their ration card. But it was questionable if the ration allowance was enough for even two good meals per day.

In February, a world food shortage had brought a return to almost wartime rations. The British government announced that the wheat content of bread was to be reduced to 1942 levels and the bread became darker. Butter, margarine and cooking fat rations were reduced and there was no hope of an increase in meat, bacon, poultry or egg supplies. There was an urgent need to feed the German people, who were threatened with famine as a result of the destruction of their agricultural industry.

A Mrs Jarrett, of Clifton Road, Hastings, complained, via the Hastings and St Leonards Observer, that there seemed to be an unfair distribution of goods around the country. On a visit to Derbyshire she saw, "ample stocks of dried egg on display for anyone to buy". She also saw on sale, non-utility furniture, car batteries, aluminium kettles, saucepans and pails. She wondered what visitors must have thought of Hastings' desolate shops. Possibly you, Angelique, were surprised at Emilie's ecstatic response to the arrival of the pot scourers but from this letter you can understand why.
(It's interesting to note that the radio programme Emilie mentions in this letter, 'The Week in Westminster", is still running in 2002.)

1946

In an attempt to combat the widespread abuse of rationing there was a nationwide police and Ministry of Food attack on food black marketers. At road blocks, vans and cars were searched for eggs, meat and poultry, which could bring more than double their fixed price, when sold under the counter; London market stalls were said to be running a flourishing trade in coupon-free clothing but it seems clothing was not a major concern to Emilie and her companions; probably the garments they had bought pre-war were built to last!

France and Holland had just started to send us vegetables again in March 1946, although the nation was still being urged to grow and eat more of their own produce, to compensate for low rations and a poor diet.

For many years, a writer contributed articles to the Hastings newspaper under the name of Vigilant, in a section called Flotsam and Jetsam; I think you will agree with me that Vigilant was male. In March 1946 he said that he, "deprecated the government plans for a June 8th 1946 Victory Parade", as he thought the public were, "not in the mood, under present circumstances". He continued, "We have already had enough interruption to the tempo of our life and the people should ask themselves, if they want both bread and circuses, where would these come from?"

The plans for celebrations, both nationally and locally, did go ahead and four Hastings lifeboat men, Muggeridge, Adams, Martin and Edmunds, marched in the London Victory Parade. Hastings had its own victory celebrations, even crusty Vigilant felt compelled to write, 'there was a spirit of widespread rejoicing and mingled thanksgiving'. The weather for the day was terrible, rain as only June can bring but it did not dampen the joy of Hastings people. Do you remember that old photo I have of the town centre, awash with rain and seawater and limp flags draped round the Albert Memorial? I think that was June 1946. To cap the month, Hastings Pier, breached and closed for the duration, re-opened for the first time since before the war.

In the winter of 1945 my parents had got a job as gardener and cook/housekeeper to a family who lived in what was to us a grand house, with a cottage for us in the grounds. It began a beneficial change in my life-style, which was to continue. We left our house on a council estate, to live among secluded lanes and woodland and expensive properties with beautiful gardens. My parents' new employer had made useful, wartime connections and this began to provide us with some of the good things that had been denied to us for years.

Love from Victoria.

1947

Lavender Cottage.   January 1st 1947.

Dear Marion,

I really don't know how to thank you for the gorgeous parcel, which has arrived quite safely. It gave me quite a thrill to open it and the contents were wonderful; you selected everything that was most needed and useful in these hard days. I don't know which I appreciated most, the cake or the eggs, the fruit or the meat, but it is no good me picking on any thing as all are very wanted things. One of my friends rhapsodised over the milk and said it must be saved for times when cream could have been used. We used to get Nestles condensed milk but that was long ago.

We intend to make a second Christmas with your parcel; the one which has just passed was so gloomy. A friend of mine had just lost her sister and her only living relatives are in America. She is very lonely so we invited her for Christmas and Boxing Days. Of course any gaiety was out of the question so now we have invited another friend, with whom we can share some of the good things you have just sent.

Things here are not very brilliant; indeed I think that we did better in wartime as regards to food. The cut in the fat ration is particularly trying, if my friend Miss Marriot were not such a good manager we should not enjoy any pastry at all. By-the-way, she is looking forward to sampling your flour. Still, I don't mean to grumble as people round here have been very kind and bring us some margarine if they can spare it.

I am wondering if Canada is snowed up yet. We have had sharp frosts and the snow round our special part has kept us indoors for some time as the corporation does nothing for the roads here. I had a few days in bed just before Christmas. I went to see an old lady in a nursing home; walking home I took a short cut through the woods and fell into a two foot deep bog. I got soaking wet and nearly ruined my dress and coat. However, a kind neighbour repaired them so no harm was done except for myself suffering slight shock. I do hope that you are keeping well and Cousin Ethel is better than she was. I'm afraid I am little confused over my address book. I have listed three for her; I trust I hit on the

right one. Again thanking you very, very much.
With love and best wishes,
Affectionately Yours, Emilie E Crane.

Footnote from Wendy: - Cousin Ethel was Wendy Johnson's grandmother (Marion Ellis' mother) who was born in 1874.

Lavender Cottage.   January 24th 1947

Dear Marion and Beatrice,

It is six years since we had such a winter as the one we are having now; my hands feel so frostbitten I can hardly write. They are wrapped in bandages so please forgive the scrawl. We are not able to go out, the snow is so deep and the Ridge has no snow plough. One of my friends has just recovered from gastric flu but the other is fairly well, if we may judge from her appetite!

Food rations are still being decreased but through a friend we did obtain two chickens and one of my National Savings Group brought us six eggs. It was good of her as she is very poor. I feel so sorry for people; some have had no coal or wood for six weeks. We sent them some of our coal but could not give much as it is rationed. There are black market buyers here and it keeps prices to a prohibitive scale, when proper organisation of supplies would feed and warm many more. We are hoarding the supplies you send us in case the food situation becomes worse. I won a pot of jam at a Boxing Day whist drive and I was pleased to bestow it on a lady who is almost blind. She cannot make her own jam and we have a fair amount of fruit from our summer garden.

I was interested in your theatrical experiences; Gielgud is one of our best actors and I remember seeing "The Importance of Being Earnest" in London. It must be thrilling to have part-ownership of a theatre. I wish we had a good one at Hastings but the only suitable building has been turned into a cinema, quite unnecessarily as there are five others. I should love to see a good play but London is too far for such a luxury.

Your mention of Niagara reminds me of my visit there with a mentally deficient but harmless young man. We sat on the edge of the falls, unromantically gnawing a cold chicken and afterwards went to the US side in, "The Maid of the Mist". We admired the view, which has now changed, I expect, as they seem to have built factories round about.

I am sorry to hear Canada has been obliged to ration its people; she has been very good to us. I must say that our present meat ration, one shilling and two pence worth per person (seven new pence) and 2 ounces of butter, are not exciting. How our friend Clare Marriott manages to make the meat last us four days is a marvel to me. It's the people who live alone who are badly hit by the meagre rations; we were able to send one of them a tin of corned beef this morning. In what must have been a reckless moment the butcher brought us one last week. The news today is not cheerful; the electricity is cut off for the day and we have neither candles nor oil, gales are expected along our coast tonight. There are others worse off, the sea is frozen at Folkestone but what can you expect at anything from 15 to 40 degrees. A village not far from here is cut off by snow and there are 250 people there with only two loaves of bread between them. The River Thames is freezing but not yet to the point where they could roast an ox on it as happened many years ago.

I must end now, the light is getting dim.

My love to you both, Emilie

Lavender Cottage.   April 4th 1947

Dear Marion and Beatrice,

Last Wednesday evening we listened to the radio to hear a speech by the Minister of Agriculture; a most gloomy account of flood damage, millions of cattle lost, the impossibility of saving crops and a consequent shortage of things one considers necessary to existence. So we went to bed somewhat downcast. In the morning our postman, still working at aged over 70, handed us a large parcel, remarking," It's heavy". I presumed it was a wireless ordered by Edith Lake for her convalescent home, but it was not. "It's from Canada!" said Clara Emily, my other friend. You should have seen our excitement; we thought we would never find an end to the things contained therein

First we hauled out a wonderful, heavy roll of ham; then jellied chicken; what a sight for sore eyes after months of considering how to share 5 wafer-thin rashers of bacon per fortnight between three people. Clara Emily, who has the role of housekeeper, pulled out one thing after another with her eyes gleaming. I don't know how to thank you. Our beef and mutton, which I suspect is horse, is mostly bones, our potatoes are damaged by frost and now only one ounce of cheese, all make for a poor table. We must not grumble; hundreds have been made homeless by floods but at 500 feet above sea level all we have is a waterlogged garden.

I am in bed with a wretched cold and my friends dodge in every minute to ask, "Are you covered up?" I am sorry that I have not posted the March edition of The Strand magazine to you but the roads were impassable with snow and ice for three weeks. The sight was magnificent; like a pantomime fairyland. Telephone wires and tree branches were coated thickly with ice; folks came up from the town just to see it. Sadly, birds died by the thousands and telephone poles crashed down into the hedges. Then the rains came and I expect you have read of the havoc that has caused. I do wonder how the farmers have the heart to carry on but the British are very resilient.

How is the weather in Canada? The only news we find of you in our papers is political. I hope you, Marion, your friend Beatrice and Cousin Ethel are managing to keep well.
Yours affectionately, Emilie

Dear Angelique,

I remember the winter of 1947 vividly, such severe, prolonged cold. The phenomenon Emilie mentions in her April 4th letter of the branches and telephone wires being coated with ice also occurred in Chislehurst in Kent, where I lived at that time. What Emilie does not

say was that as the ice-coated branches moved against each other in the icy wind they made an eerie, glassy clatter. I was rather frightened as it seemed like the end of the world; I felt that spring could never come again.

At the end of January, snow storms struck Hastings, which was swept with north-easterly winds and blizzard conditions, the worst for years. Snow lay six to twelve inches deep everywhere and there were shoulder-high snowdrifts on the seaward-facing West Hill. The hilly nature of Hastings often meant that public transport was reduced or stopped because of the dangerous roads.

There was no let up on the austerity drive, even in those bitterly cold months. Hastings people were urged to save more fuel; the gas company asked the public to economise, coal merchants would not deliver supplies to householders who already had a month's stock; cinemas opened later; street lighting was reduced and shops were lit by candles, night lights and hurricane lamps. The Hastings Town Crier was used to make public announcements about the fuel crisis. If this all sounds romantic; snow-clad streets, log fires, candle-lit shops, believe me, it wasn't.

Britain was in danger of being brought to its knees; all over the country heavy snowstorms and sub-zero temperatures prevented trains from delivering coal, which in turn caused power cuts. How thankful we were at home for my mother's steaming vegetable soup and the firewood my father had collected from do-not-ask-where! In these wretched weeks we did not go anywhere; my parents' live-in job as cook and gardener-handy man meant they did not have to travel to work but for those who were obliged to do so it was a nightmare. Transport all over the country was seriously disrupted and emergency regulations added to the confusion.

Food was in short supply and troops had to be called in to combat a further blow to the country; a road haulage strike. In London there were long queues at butchers' shops, some sold out and greengrocers rationed customers to two pounds of potatoes per customer. The fresh meat ration was reduced from 1/2d (6p) worth to 1/- (5p) per week, a cut in bread ration was predicted as wheat stocks were low; this led to a 50% reduction in beer production. Not much risk of obesity or drunkenness then, as you will gather!

When the thaw came it brought a new disaster; floods. Two million sheep were drowned and 500,000 acres of wheat ruined, which represented a month's bread supply for the nation. For smokers like Emilie, the final blow was the increase of a packet of 20 cigarettes from 2/4d to 3/4d, (12p to17p).

You have remarked, Angelique, that you were astonished by the pre-occupation of the Lavender Cottage household with food, you are now probably beginning to understand the importance of the goodies sent to the three elderly women and why they were so grateful.

In July 1947, the elder of my two brothers was married and I was one of the bridesmaids. My mother made my dress from some hard to come by pink, crepe fabric and I was allowed to wear make-up for the day; I was twelve and a half. I discovered that a wedding, apart from anything else, is a great piece of theatre and I was thrilled to have a minor, starring role, though you would never guess it from the scowl on my face in the photographs.

There now follows another big gap in Emilie's letters; it certainly cannot be the fault of the elderly, Lavender Cottage postman, who seemed to get the post through come what may. A contemporary report said that even during the worst of the winter of 1947, the post was still delivered in Hastings.
Love from Victoria

Lavender Cottage.   Oct 16th 1947

Dear Marion and Beatrice,

The gorgeous box of soap arrived and we were absolutely thrilled! What a quantity, we shall certainly be clean for a twelvemonth.

1947

Sunlight soap we haven't seen for months, Palmolive, an imitation only and as for Lux, well, I believe we did have a packet a year ago. In any case we haven't seen any good soap for many months so you may guess how welcome it is. The strawberries and peach jam will be a blessing, the label mentioned dried eggs, butter and fats but we did not see how you could have put them in with the soap without them picking up the scent; the parcel was so firmly packed.

You will think that I am a disgraceful person to get ill again but I am writing this in bed. I have a bronchial cold with head pains and sickness. I feel I am a nuisance but Clare Emily makes no trouble of it. The doctor was not very cheerful as he was starting an illness, now his son tells me his father has pneumonia badly. It seems to be a wide spread complaint here; they say that the drought is causing much illness. Things are pretty restless all round; it would not surprise me if another election arrived before its time. Sorry to send such a dull letter, perhaps I will be better soon and not so addle-headed.
With love to you both, Emilie

Lavender Cottage.   Nov 18th   1947

Dear Marion,

This is not a letter but just an acknowledgement of yours, which was so exciting that when I read out the list of the contents of your forthcoming parcel, Clare Emily was so overcome she had to sit down. You may imagine how we shall watch for the postman in his red van as he nears the cottage. He is very nice and so sympathetic when something comes that looks interesting.

Did you listen to the Royal Wedding? (Princess Elizabeth and Prince Phillip) I felt sorry for the thousands who sat out in the streets all night to watch the morning's procession. They wrapped themselves in newspapers to keep out the cold.
My love to you and Beatrice
Yours, Emilie.

1947

Lavender Cottage.   December 5th 1947.

My Dear Marion,

Please forgive me for not having written earlier but I hope my letter will reach you in time for Christmas greetings. It has been a very trying year with illness here and among friends-one of 60 years standing died after much suffering, a fortnight ago. I have spent much time during the year visiting her and her sister. My two friends here have been ill and I have done my part in that respect also. I think it must have been the lack of sunshine that has affected most people. Never has there been such a bad summer-and the rain! The wheat suffered terribly and if it had not been for Canada I do not know where we should have been. Your country has been so helpful and kind in many ways.

It did seem strange for our bread to be rationed; we were used to a shortage of milk, meat, eggs, biscuits, etc, but when it came to bread, well, I hope we didn't grumble too much! I'm afraid many people spend their bread units (rations) on cakes at which my friend here was most indignant. She said 'Can't they make their own cakes?' I wonder they don't, for the bought cakes are uncommonly short of fruit-the sultanas really needed telephonic communication if they are anxious to talk to each other. I don't know how people will manage about Christmas pudding but we shall get a home made one. My friend is an excellent manager and has turned out some good cakes and biscuits; how she does it on one ounce of fat per head I don't know. Well, that's enough of food, though it is the main topic in every conversation. You may begin quite a serious talk on the political situation or the latest book but in the end it's always what we eat or don't eat.

I enclose a copy of The Strand in default of any better publication. They say things are improving in this respect but I haven't noticed it. Someone gave me a ticket for Boots Library but all the new books are printed in such small type that my eyes won't read it and if the printing is good the price is sinful. If you have any time please drop me a line and say how you all are. Excuse this writing paper, I can't recommend it!
Affectionately Yours,
Emilie.

1947

Lavender Cottage.   December 15th 1947.

Dear Marion and Beatrice,

What gorgeous parcels! Out first came two tins of delicious bacon on
which we fell tooth and nail. Rations of two thin slices per fortnight
per person have not given us much scope. Later, there arrived a
weighty parcel which I carried up to Clare Emily's bedroom, she
having retired with lumbago and a heavy cold, all at once. However
she is much better, I'm sure that the parcel had a beneficial effect; you
should have seen her gloat over it. The dried fruit especially appealed
to her housewifely mind, so of course we had to start making the
Christmas pudding at once.

I begged from her half the sugar, intending to make some parsnip wine
but I felt Clare Emily thought this rather wasteful. You can imagine her
rapture over the dried fruit as the distribution here is very scanty. The
grocer is always very apologetic, "So sorry no dates or sultanas this
month, we may have some in for Christmas". But he didn't. You even
thought to send bay leaves and cloves, both a curiosity as we have not
seen them for some time. Edith Lake has cast very wistful eyes at the
cake you sent; you can't keep her off cake if there happens to be one
in the offing. I helped her make her pudding yesterday because she has
become so forgetful and I am sure she would have left out the suet. The
butcher actually sent us some, he is a nice kind man, even if his meat
is leathery, but that is not his fault.

The one person who did not appreciate the parcel was James our cat
who is thirteen. I have promised him a bit of salmon one day. He is a
spoilt wretch and will not eat meat unless it has onion-flavoured gravy.
He really prefers frozen cod, a mercy, as fish is the only un-rationed
food. James is well but his temper is variable and if the fish is not fresh
he mentions it fluently. He is only a common tabby tom but well
marked and very loving when good tempered.

To my delight your third, weighty parcel contained cheese; I have
already nibbled it and look forward to Welsh Rarebit tonight, quite
oblivious to indigestion. We don't know how to thank you and
Beatrice. Clare Emily says you are trumps and I feel almost sinful at

being so fortunate. EL does not get any nice things sent, except for a salmon her rich sister bestows on her occasionally, in the summer, but we always share our things with Edith. CE's brother-in-law is very kind though not rich. He always brings us baskets of apples and her brother is very good in sending us cigarettes, also her nephew.

This reminds me, you kindly asked about cigarettes but I do get quite a number given me and I smoke more than I should. C E's relatives are all very good, though they are not wealthy. It is odd that rich people are never as generous as those who are hard up; I suppose it is a fellow feeling. I do wish I had something nice you would like but I do not know your tastes. Cousin Ethel sent me a very pretty Christmas card. I am a bit late with mine owing to my stupid illness.

Yours affectionately, Emilie.

PS Oh the cranberry jelly! I have not seen any since we were in Canada.

Lavender Cottage.   December 27th 1947

Dear Marion and Beatrice

I had just found my fountain pen, which I often lose, when your letter arrived; I am so woolly-headed from a nasty attack of flu. The main subject of this epistle to you was to be the HAM. It deserves capital letters and many acknowledgements. We did manage to get a fowl for Christmas at a not too exorbitant price, it looked very white and nice and promised a typical Christmas dinner. I got out of my sick-bed to boil it; it's never safe to roast anything these days. I always have the honour of cooking Christmas dinner. Well, I never tasted a worse bird, it was so leathery our forks refused to penetrate its hide and it ended in soup. Said Clar'Emily, "Never mind, we've got the ham" Indeed it is lovely ham. She cooked part of it and it was delicious; it has already provided dinners and suppers for days. The larger piece sits in the larder and will last no end of time.

I'm sure you don't mind but we gave our neighbour some samples of the butter, lard and cheese from your parcel. She is so good in doing our shopping and helping with our home nursing, that we are glad to be able help her out with some food. Rationing is particularly hard on single people. We will not eat your Christmas pudding until a friend, ill at present, can share it with us. EL cannot wait to be let loose on the cake, she is a wolf for anything sweet.

I could discourse on the food for pages but I had better proceed to our ménage, as you kindly enquired about it. When I left the office, where I was managing a department for a Scholastic Agency after WWI, Edith Lake, a friend living at Sutton, came down to Hastings with her mother and was anxious for us to make our home here also. She bought us a bungalow, which I think you saw, where we had quite a nice home. When her mother died Edith wanted to come and live with us but the bungalow was too small so she sold it and between us we bought this house. Later she returned us the money we had paid, to avoid difficulties if anything happened to her.

So now we pay her a modest rent, as she is very kind. I forgot to say that she built on to this house as it was also too small. Things are all right as long as EL keeps well but her head is very bad, she cannot remember anything and the doctor says her brain arteries are hardening. It will be a bad day when she goes but I expect something will turn up, it always does.

We all live together on account of the heating. EL has a maid who is supposed to come all day but is under treatment at the hospital, so she goes after lunch. CE does all the cooking, though she sometimes lets me take a hand but not often as she says we might be fairly well fed on Monday but Friday would find an empty larder! I'm sure that's a slander. We have a 75 year-old char, who comes in for two hours; I can't say that she is much of a cleaner but she has walked over two miles through rain and snow during 14 years so we are thankful for her. Maids demand £2.00.00 to £3.15.00 per week and won't sleep in.

We also have a kind of gardener between us who gives us a day and a half per week but we can't pay him the average wage, which runs into 16 shillings to 18 shillings (80 to 90 pence) per day now. Still, he is quite good, though he does not always arrive, but he gets in coal and wood for us.

Well you will be bored stiff if I keep on. We would very much like to know if you don't mind telling us, how old you are (very impolite of us). Clar'Emily is 76 Edith Lake is 77 and I shall be 77 in February. James the cat is thirteen and very expensive to keep but he is a dear. If you could send us a photograph of yourself we would be glad. Otherwise, ask Beatrice to make a sketch of you, I'm sure she could do it. Sorry this letter is jerky, my friends are both talking at the same time and I do not know what I am writing.I am glad to hear Cousin Ethel can travel.

Yours affectionately, Emilie.

Dear Angelique,

Wasn't it interesting to read about Emilie's life, her companions, how they came together and the all-important cat, James? I have to identify him as a cat because he is written about in such loving terms you might mistakenly think he was a brother! I visualise Edith Lake as a little pampered and spoiled, perhaps lacking the confidence that her two career women friends had developed. In spite of the problems of old age and illness, Emilie remains cheerful. I love her generosity and optimism, two characteristics that sadly, contributed to her later misfortunes. The Beatrice in the letter's salutation is Marion's house companion and they were, as Emilie and Clara had been, working women, but much younger. I agree with you, reading all the "foody" details makes one feel hungry. Isn't it splendid to see how generous Emilie was in times of scarcity, sharing the good things with friends and neighbours?

It was partly the distance of Lavender Cottage from the town that made it so difficult for its occupants to get domestic help, added to social and economic changes that had come about since the end of the war. In 1942 a local newspaper advertisement for a domestic offered a comfortable home and 25/- (£1.25) per week to a capable, live-in cook/general, in the household of a Hastings jeweller. Five years later, according to Emilie, a housemaid, "demanded £2.00.00 to £3.15.00 (£3.75) per week".

1947

The summer of 1947 had seen the introduction of new austerity cuts, and, as the nation's crisis increased, the compulsory direction of workers to essential services, in operation during the war, was reconsidered. In recognition of their importance to the nation, miners, farmers and fishermen were allowed bigger rations of meat, cheese and eggs.

Her later letters reveal that Emilie was not much interested in clothes but she must have read about Christian Dior's "New Look". After years of wartime restrictions on fabric and clothing manufacture, the new fashion used yards of material in long, full skirted costumes. Fashion-starved women fell in love with the new style; one London store sold 700 suits in two weeks. The government asked women to ignore the fashion for longer skirts, to save fabric, in the national interest. My cousin, who was a good needle woman, made her self a "new look" dress from an artificial silk bedspread; I thought she looked very elegant!

The glittering, royal wedding really was a tonic. We were so weary of austerity and it was just what the people needed at that time. I remember the newspaper pictures of the huddles of spectators who had slept on pavements overnight, reserving the best spots, to see the wedding procession. Princess Elizabeth's dress, by Norman Hartnell, was embroidered with beads and pearls and she wore a diamond circlet to hold her veil in place. This was the first time I and many others had seen a royal occasion on television; we were invited into the "big house" to watch events on the television set of my parents' employers. The government had given the Princess extra clothing coupons for her wedding dress but she decided to go on honeymoon without a trousseau, owing to the clothing shortage.

The austerity spirit was still very much in evidence in Hastings, demonstrated when the Chief Constable, Lt Colonel A G Cargill, refused a licence extension for the Royal Victoria Hotel dinner dance, to celebrate the royal wedding. He said: "Those who wish to pay their respects to the royal couple can quite easily drink their health before 10:00pm!" The royal wedding certainly brought a feeling of celebration to the town; flags fluttered from the Albert Memorial, hotels and public buildings, shops had red, white and blue displays, some featured bridal gowns. The Ritz and Regal Cinemas opened to allowed the public to enter free of charge to listen to a broadcast of the marriage ceremony; there were large audiences. Restaurants served what they called wedding lunches and they put slices of wedding cake on the tea tables. Where did they get the ingredients, I wonder? Perhaps it was from the spivs!

In December 1947, the government pushed through an order to defeat, "spivs and drones". A spiv was a man who made a living by various disreputable dealings, existing by his wits rather than holding down any job. He was a small-time crook, living on the fringes of real criminality. You must have seen the spiv character in Dads' Army on television. The spiv was most strongly associated with the period during and immediately after the Second World War in Britain; he always seemed able to get those coveted luxury items that were unobtainable in that period of austerity, except on the black market. Drones are male bees whose sole purpose in the hive is to mate with the queen, they are fat and lazy and produce nothing, hence the reference!

As Christmas approached the Hastings butchers were told by the Ministry of Food that there would be no pork for the ration, even the Lavender Cottage chicken proved to be a disappointment. The hotels in the town were surprisingly well booked for the holiday, even though some hoteliers feared that the low, basic petrol ration would keep visitors away.

Boxing Day brought brilliant sunshine and cloudless blue skies, after a Christmas Day of high winds and rain; people were strolling along the seafront or sitting in the promenade shelters. It was concluded that in spite of austerity most people had a good time. Even dour 'Vigilant' wrote that there was no rationing of fun and kindness. For my family, it was our last Christmas in Chislehurst, before moving to Hastings and to a way of life which cushioned us from the worst effects of the continuing austerity.
Love from Victoria.

1948

Lavender Cottage.   January 18th 1948

Dear Marion and Beatrice,

The suet and beef arrived quite safely and was declared by Clar'Em'ly to be the best meat we had tasted since 1940. I know you won't mind me having given samples to two single neighbours who each get only one shilling's-worth (5p) of meat per week. You see our poor cattle don't get the food now and so they produce only exceedingly tough flesh, devoid of fat. People can't get anything to make up for it. Whatever doctors in the newspapers say, our own doctors tell us frankly that the population, except possibly the black market users, is not properly nourished, hence so much illness.

We are very fortunate to have people like you who think of us as you do; we all send you warmest thanks. E L does not eat meat as a rule but she has been enjoying the pies. We have a neighbour who lets us have one or two eggs when her hens lay, just because I take her parrot sweets now and then. The parrot, called Laura, is 30 years old, a disreputable old bird whose language can not be repeated, but she is the apple of her missus' eye.

The prediction of further austerity by Mr Strachey, the Minister of Food has not worried us too much. I do feel it was a great mistake not to put a ceiling on wages. The workers in some cases are paid extravagant wages and as they can't get food, they buy stupid luxuries and save nothing. I believe in good wages but there are limits! However I must not talk politics, because I know little of economics I am not a competent judge. I am so sorry, I am sure I sent the January Strand some time back but perhaps I forgot so I will send another. Give the spare to a friend if I sent two.

With much love, Emilie.

Dear Angelique,

As you can see austerity still dominated life in Lavender Cottage, I was interested to discover that in December 1947 a 600lb food consignment, sent from Canada to Hastings, had been made up into 74 individual parcels and distributed to local ex-serviceman and the elderly. So, it was not just the ladies at Lavender Cottage who were benefiting from Canadian generosity. There is a firm link between Hastings and Canada; so many local people emigrated there at the turn of the 20th century and after the First World War.

The New Year, Mayoral Banquet was cancelled but the long tradition of the Old Town Winkle Club charity fund-raising dinner went ahead, after a run-in with the Minister of Food about the guest list exceeding the statutory 100. It was later announced, to laughter, in the House of Commons, by the Minister of Food, Mr Strachey, that the permission for dinner was a mistake and should never have taken place. You cannot call back 200 eaten dinners; trust those wily fishermen to get the better of a government department!

People were still being asked to save fuel, especially electricity, between 7:00am and 7:00pm. There was very little industry in Hastings but that which there was, organised night shifts, to spread the load.

The controversy that surrounded the setting up of the National Health Service was beginning to appear; medical consultants and specialists in the London area voted by 766 to 11 to reject service under the National Health Act. A leading surgeon said that doctors would become paid servants, without a say, in an administration run by civil servants.
Love from Victoria.

Lavender Cottage.   16th February 1948

Dear Marion and Beatrice,

I am sorry not to have written for some time but things have been a little awkward.

I don't think that I told you that EL is the secretary to a convalescent home, which has been in a pack of trouble since Christmas, with shortage of staff, which has necessitated many letters and enquiries. Reports also have to be prepared for the Annual Meeting and extra committee meeting held. Poor EL's head has been so bad she could not do any of the work but it would so grieve her to give up after 17 years, so I have had to do it and at the same time try to convince her that she is still the secretary.

The Annual meeting is next week and she wants to read the report but the poor dear can't speak without stuttering so I don't know what will happen. There is a blessed Countess coming to the meeting, an old lady who speaks in a whisper. We have put EL to bed and have sent for the doctor, not that he can do much.

It was interesting to hear about your work. Fancy Beatrice being a drama critic; perhaps she could get a copy of the London Free Press for us to see. We did not know that you both worked but imagined you to be ladies of leisure. This makes your kindnesses to us much more striking. EL was very touched by your message and she will appreciate the apricots and peaches. The serge fabric has not arrived yet. I expect the customs are considering keeping it; but I shall have a word to say on that point.

CM sends her love and thanks, she has never tasted maple syrup but she would like to do so. Also she says that a little ground allspice would be very acceptable, what we get has no flavour. We so enjoyed the contents of your last parcel; bacon, butter, beef; CM was riotous over the sultanas! One neighbour went mad over the cheese, another over the salmon; it was so nice to be able to give them a treat. I must end now and go and feed EL with slippery elm, which is very light and nourishing.
Yours affectionately, Emilie.

Dear Angelique,

I felt ridiculously thrilled to find a report of the 1948 Catherine House AGM in the flimsy, yellowing pages of the local paper. The establishment was described as a "Convalescent Home for Gentlewomen". Never hear that word now; perhaps today's female senior citizens are too outspoken and brazen to justify it!

The report names the President, Countess Brassey and a Miss Crane, who was acting as Hon: Sec: in place of Miss Lake (Miss?), who was absent through illness. The Chairman, Mrs Beasley reminded the committee that Miss Lake had been their secretary for 16 years, including during the war; birthday greetings were sent to the home's patroness, Princess Alice Countess of Athlone. The article also informs that the finances of the home are in a poor state. I telephoned the home, which still exists at 57, Church Road, St Leonards on Sea; it has another name now and a youthful management. There was no interest shown in my enquiry about old records or archives; a pity.

It looks as if a crack-down on spivs was working; in February a local man was fined £30, huge sum then, for conducting a black market deal for 56lbs of butter and 7lbs of lard; he had paid £14.00 for the butter and £1.00 for the lard.

There was still strong feeling by doctors against the NHS; in a British Medical Association poll, 86 % of doctors voted against joining the National Health Service.
Elderly aunts in my family decided to hang on to their chronic symptoms in the hopes of getting free NHS treatment.
Love from Victoria.

Lavender Cottage.   March 2nd 1948

Dear Marion and Beatrice,

The skirt arrived on the 26th of February and what a lovely parcel! The serge is beautiful; strange to relate the customs don't seem to have opened it.   Any way they have not sent a bill. All the making accessories included too. I am sending it away to my dressmaker because she makes things so much better than any one here. CM went wild over the towels and face flannels; there is rather a distinct shortage of these in the house and I exalted over the handkerchiefs. Our old cleaning lady, who washes mine, is very tired of having old bits of sheets handed to her; she says that it is time I had some respectable hankies when I go visiting. The little lady-shaped needle-holder is very nice, you think of everything don't you?

Today I found that our last year's potatoes had been frosted so I had to throw away about 20 pounds to save the others. The snow has gone now and we are thinking of sowing seeds but the 500 feet altitude on the Ridge means it is colder here than in town.

I ought to have acknowledged your parcel earlier but EL has been very ill again and is only just out of bed. The annual meeting at the convalescent home was on Wednesday, but as EL was in bed I had to write her report and act as secretary. Our own church meeting came on Saturday; I am secretary for that too and another report had to be written. I am glad both meetings are over. EL is resigning from the home's committee next week and I just know that they will elect me.

The trying part is that the government is taking over all the hospitals and most of the convalescent homes and we do not know whether ours will go too and that means a pile of correspondence. I wish they would let us alone as we get on very well and the people are glad of it as the fees are low and everything is very nice.

The newspapers make ghastly reading, don't they? Poor Czechoslovakia; we feel rather scared as Russia's power is getting so extensive and some folks anticipate another war. But it is no good dwelling on that and we must go on as well as possible and thank heaven for our kind friends beyond the seas.
Yours affectionately, Emilie.

Dear Angelique,

Always, concerned with food, Emilie grieves her frosted potatoes. The winter of '48 was not as severe as the previous year; the first snow did not arrive till 19th February but a thaw set in after a few hours, followed by a heavy frost then snow again, which lay deeply. The height of the Ridge meant that winter was worse there and hung about longer there than in other parts of the town; Emilie's potatoes bear witness!

1948

Things were much worse for the population of Europe, as can be discerned from a letter in the local paper that begged for money, "to buy relief supplies from Australia in the form of shark liver oil, lard, dried and skimmed milk, herrings in brine and orange juice for the children and elderly in refugee and displaced person's camps".

The "ghastly news" to which Emilie refers was when, on 27th February, the communists seized power in Czechoslovakia. Mass rallies were organised by the communists to support an un-named government. The hopes of those who opposed the Communists rested with Jan Masaryk, aged 61, Foreign Minister and son of the late and respected president. It seemed that the peace people longed for would never materialize.
Love from Victoria.

Lavender Cottage.   March 8th 1948.

Dear Marion and Beatrice,
Re Parrot:
I went over to see her this evening and found her mistress, Mrs Todd, very distressed as the bird has rheumatism in one foot and had declined her food. I don't wonder, as it was positive rubbish. I gave your kind message and Mrs Todd was most grateful. She said, "If only I could get a little good seed for her I'm sure she would do better". So I promised to write at once. Perhaps if you could send a little seed for her she would indeed be better. Mrs Todd is all alone and Laura is a good companion when fit. This evening she was like Pet Marjorie's duck, "She was most uncommon ca'm and never said a single damn".But as I left I did hear a remark from the bird, it sounded like, "blast yer", but I trust I was mistaken!

I liked your description of the summer place at Ipperwash, it sounds delightful; it must be handy to have a car to get about in. We do have cars now and then as EL cannot go any distance without one but CE and I take buses mostly.

I have not heard from the customs re the serge fabric, perhaps they have forgotten me. We are so grateful for the milk you sent us; this week our ration was cut to one third of a pint each and as we must give EL most of it was a great joy to open a tin. She is still very poorly but we hope to get her out of bed this week. Mrs Todd told me that she has used up all her tea ration for the next day. As we are all over 70 we get an extra ration. It is rough on some people as tea seems to be their only drink. We always have spare tea to offer to a neighbour. A chatty neighbour has just floated in and I don't know what I am writing now and it is becoming a scrawl.

Yours affectionately, Emilie.

Dear Angelique,

I love the terse opening to the letter; Laura the parrot is certainly a character; I would so like to know the origin of the quote concerning Pet Marjorie's duck; the Internet yields nothing helpful. It seems that Emilie and her companions did not go into town very often. It was not just old age and the weather that kept them at home. The Ridge bus service was very poor (as now!) and public transport was probably a bit tricky for those not too steady on their feet. Contemporary letters in the local paper complained about the jerky stops and starts of the buses and the hazard these posed to the elderly and infirm. You can gather there were cars to hire but petrol was in short supply. This was causing local and national concern among those in the holiday trade and a group of all-party MPs pleaded for petrol concessions, to help the plight of seaside and holiday towns.

Emilie does not mention the situation in Czechoslovakia again but two days after this letter was written, Jan Masaryk was found lying dead in a courtyard beneath his flat in the foreign office. Prague Radio announced his death as a suicide, whilst suffering from a nervous breakdown. His supporters did not accept this verdict; Masaryk was seen as the last opponent to the communist take over and the announcement caused international dismay.

I do not want to take Emilie's story too far from home and only include items like this either when she has mentioned them or they are relevant to local life. Even within these limitations, Emilie is improving my modern history no end!
Love from Victoria

1948

Lavender Cottage.   April 5th 1948.

Dear Marion and Beatrice,

A most lovely ham has just arrived. The date of postage is March 31st so it took only five days to come by air. The ham is the nicest we have has since before the war and we have shared it with an invalid friend and Mrs Todd, our neighbour, who does shopping for us.

In your letter of 27th you said you would send butter; may we be saucy and ask for sugar too? We made ten pots of marmalade with your last consignment and would like to make jam from the blackcurrants in the garden when they ripen, if they do. The weather is so variable this year, the poor plants can't stand up to it. I hope yours is more stable.

EL has had another short bout of illness and her mind is very strange. She has at last obtained some wool and is going to make baby clothes so that will keep her busy.

James, the cat, is rather cross because the fishmonger can supply only plaice, which is very unsubstantial, and we cannot allow him more than half a plaice per meal. Mrs Todd is very happy to hear she might get some seed from you for the parrot. I took the bird, Laura, a bone last week but even that did not please her. She emitted a number of remarks that sounded uncommonly like "damns".

We are anxiously awaiting Stafford Cripps' budget tomorrow and we are hoping for no more cuts. The bacon and cheese rations are only one and half ounces now so you may imagine how welcome your ham is. No news from the excise people, so I conclude that they are not going to say anything about the skirt and serge fabric etc.
Yours affectionately, Emilie

1948

Dear Angelique,

No wonder Emilie feared further cuts in food rations, in March the government had announced a cut in the cheese ration from two ounces to one and a half ounces per week per person. It was plain that austerity was far from over when, in April, the Fuel Minister, Hugh Gaitskill, said that motorists would be rationed to 90 miles per month from June.

In my family, on April 18th 1948, came an upheaval that transformed our lives; my parents' employers moved us, with them, from Chislehurst in Kent to a farm in Fairlight, just outside Hastings. Chislehurst was a pretty place; big houses and lots of common land but nothing had prepared me for the idyllic loveliness of that little farm, in a lush, green valley, seen for the first time on a perfect, flower-filled spring day. Easter fell on April 3rd in 1948 but as there was a ban on leisure motoring people mostly travelled to Hastings by train or coach. In spite of this, hotels and boarding houses had plenty of bookings and the town saw 40,000 visitors.

Political and administrative skirmishes continued in the run up to the founding of the NHS, Aneurin Bevan offered doctors freedom of partnership and practice under the National Health Service. April 26th was the celebration of the Silver wedding of King George and Queen Elizabeth; I do not recall any events to mark this but there was a special postage stamp issued. I saw recently that one of these, in mint condition, is now worth £38!
Love from Victoria.

Lavender Cottage.   May 19th 1948

My Dear Marion,

We are feeling a bit worried as we have not heard from you for a long time. It is not a question of your kindness in sending us such nice things. But I have the idea that one of you may be ill. I do hope that this is not the case. I should be glad of a line or just a card. It may be that your letters are lost; so many things are going astray these days.

We are going on all right. The weather is so fine that the gardens are drying up; I'm sure it can't be hotter with you. The only person who is not up to the mark is James who is very limp and off his food. It occurred to me it may be Cousin Ethel who is ill and that you are both very busy, but I won't anticipate anything unpleasant. Please give us a short epistle. I have been gardening all day and feel like a rag.
Yours affectionately, Emilie.

Dear Angelique,

No wonder Emilie felt like a rag; it was very hot for May. The water in the St Leonards open air bathing pool (since demolished) was 67 degrees. It seems that life had been hotting-up generally; maternity wards and home midwives all over the country were busy as figures showed that the birth rate was the highest in the UK for 26 years. This was ascribed to couples 'catching up' on the lost war years and decreased infant mortality. In June, Princess Elizabeth joined the baby-boom; it was announced that she was expecting a baby in the autumn.

Twelve extra clothing coupons per person were available from May until the end of September; I wonder what Emilie and her friends did with theirs? For those less clothes conscious they were a useful form of currency. For my family, living on a farm meant the virtual end of many aspects of austerity. Suddenly there was plenty of dairy produce and the meat ration was supplemented with freshly caught rabbits, delicious! (I loathe it now).

An incredible story came from the Hastings newspaper dated May 22nd 1948. The Hastings Food Control Committee mentioned complaints that corned mutton sent from Australia tasted of iodine. Although the Sanitary Inspector described the meat as unpalatable, due to excess preservative, the public were asked to eat it anyhow to help the butchers out! Can you imagine that today?
Over 10,000 doctors, more than half the total, had relented and joined

the National Health Service after government reassurances. You will see however from Emilie's next letter that the NHS facilities were not handed out liberally to everyone,
Love from Victoria.

Lavender Cottage.　　　11th June 1948.

My Dear Marion,

We were very pleased to have your letter, and to hear you were keeping well. I can quite understand your talk of 'laziness' as all here seem to have felt rather limp - it has been more than usually warm in this part of the world, and one gets so sleepy. We are feeling somewhat cross at the absence of rain; every other part of England has had quite a bit, but we have been favoured only with a couple of showers, and the garden is so parched I don't believe a vegetable will survive. Of course one ought not to grouse, as the holiday folk have had a good time, but it is a trifle wearing. Even James is unlike his usual self, and allows the birds to come within a yard of him. Evidently, though, you have not had the weather we have, but have changed over with us.

We have kept very well, all of us, but Clar' Emly would be cross if she heard me say that, as she always thinks I am in for pneumonia these warm months, and after three experiences she gets nervous - won't let us go for a holiday this year, as I disgraced myself the last two years at this season! Of course we could go down to the beach, but it is so crowded nowadays that we find the garden preferable. I have been trying to grow some sweet corn, the remains of seeds brought from Canada, but of course they are very, very old, and only one survived. However, he is doing his best, and as the others don't appreciate the corn, it doesn't much matter.

We are still enjoying the soap, etc., you sent us. My skirt is not made up yet, as our pet dress-maker got married, and doesn't do much work, but she has promised to do it for me. I am still puzzled about the Customs - they have not sent in any claim for it so far. And I cherish the hankies - only on very specials occasions does one issue forth. Our old 'char' washes the others - she did about 100 last month, and remarked, 'Well, I dunno what you do with them there 'anks, Miss Crane - I s'pose you've bin a cleaning up your spades with 'em!', which is exceedingly likely. She is a real character. She comes for 3 hours per week, and her arrival is signalised by a sound of bombs and the hasty departure of James for the bottom of the garden. But she is a treasure in these days, when a morning maid wants 3 pounds a week. She is over 70 and has her pension, but will not leave us, comes through rain, hail and snow, and never asks for a penny more - of course we give her extra now, but not at her request. I did some distempering last week; she didn't think much of it (no more did I!) and frankly informed me it "wasn't much to be proud of". I expect your painting is more effective.

You and Beatrice seem to have had some hard work of late, and I don't wonder you felt "lazy". It would be interesting to know how far you are from your office, and, by the way, we should like to see some of Beatrice's articles - perhaps you could send a copy of the paper, but perhaps it is a too expensive one.

I must tell you again how much the ham was enjoyed, not only by ourselves. There is a young man, a cripple from the war, to whom I take tobacco now and then. I took him and his wife a piece and told them about you and Beatrice. They said they had not tasted anything like it for long before the last war. Our neighbour, too, was quite excited over it, and hoarded it to give titbits to visitors. She is a very kind woman, who does most of our shopping for us.

Clar' Emly wants to know whether there will be a chance of seeing you some day - I hope there will, but I know how expensive the fares are now. It would be nice if you and Beatrice could come. The niece of my friend in the Nursing Home may come over in September - she is at Salt Lake City. I wish she could do so, as her Aunt is a problem, a mental case. She writes me letters every day. Yesterday I had one, telling me the niece had come, and she would see her the next day. As I had a note from the girl last week, and she wrote from Salt Lake, this was hard to believe! I go to see the Aunt every Tuesday, and she begs me to take her to her own home, but the doctor says she must remain where she is. She has no relatives this side, so one can't do much for her. Excuse this rigmarole. I haven't any more of this thin paper, but hope you can read my scrawl. Much love to you and Beatrice, and take care of yourselves - don't work too hard. Yours, Emilie.

1948

Lavender Cottage.   July 23rd 1948.

Dear Marion and Beatrice,

Thank you very much for the papers. We were most interested in Beatrice's article; there was a pleasing dry humour in it which amused us greatly. Clar' Em'ly was especially taken with the remarks on 'Shirley' as she had only just finished reading it for about the tenth time and it was good to see old Isaak remembered.

My curiosity was aroused by the reference to 'railroad cake'. I looked through a torn and tattered cookery book I brought from Guelph years back, but it was not given there. It sounds a bit hard and steely to me.

I take it 'Angels' was also from Beatrice's pen. I wish that I could write articles and have them appear in public. I did once come out in The Times with a scholastic letter and also with a play in the 'Boy's Own Paper" but that is way back.

We are going on as usual; weeks of drizzling rain have been succeeded by a heat wave and the garden has just dried up. James, the cat is suffering from an excess of fur. At present he is endeavouring to flatten the onions, finding some coolness in their contact. Probably later, when I require it done, he will sit on the rising celery! The wind has devastated our apples, which lie on the earth in an unripe condition. Clar' Em'ly made an apple charlotte of them today; it wasn't bad and as bread is no longer rationed, this was easy.

From my sowing, only one sweet corn has survived, but I should not grumble as the seed was old, from Canada, ages ago. The birds have eaten nearly all the pea seeds, in spite of the discouragement of stringing them with threads of black cotton, but the Canadian Wonder beans are lively and we hope to pick some next week.

I expect you have heard something about our new National Health Service. I tried to get the free medical advice, but our doctor declined to take me as a 'panel' patient and Clar' Em'ly thinks it is best, as she says that I am bound to get pneumonia and then might want him in a hurry. The radio therapist is on strike and as he has a monopoly here it is no use grumbling. This scheme is very hard on the middle classes, who get so few concessions, but of course there is always some hitch with sweeping reforms.

I wonder if you are spending the weekends at your country house. From your letter it sounds lovely though you do have a good deal of painting to do. It must be nice for you not to have such long working hours now. A five thirty end to your work could not have left you much time when you had meals to get afterwards. I expect it is as difficult for you to get maids as it is for us here. EL has one for the mornings but has to pay double salary now for the same hours.

We still have the old char who comes for 4 hours a week and will not retire. She says she, 'Don't want no more money' but we do give her a little extra. She has her pension and says she is well off now. It is good working people here are better off. They have had a bad deal in the past but one can't help feeling things are a little overdone as the high wages send up prices tremendously. Clar' Em'ly says that I must go and water the garden now as it's getting shady.
Yours affectionately, Emilie.

Dear Angelique,

What lovely, long chatty letters these are. Local news items bear out Emilie's reference to a heat wave. Fridges in businesses all over the town broke down, unable to cope with the extreme temperatures; it was 89 in the shade. I was amused to learn that the Hastings Chief Constable, warned residents and visitors of the dangers of too much sunshine. Oh happy days, when the police had the time to concern themselves with such homely things!

Austerity seemed to be loosening a little, brighter street lighting was permitted but the Electricity and Public Lighting Committee said that public lighting restrictions would not allow ornamental lights on the promenade bandstand. (Yes, I know, another grandly named committee, wouldn't today's borough councillors just love it?) A further sign of the easing of austerity was that the government announced the end of rationing of footwear and furnishing fabrics by 9th September 1948.

On 5th July the National Health Service came into being, along with a national insurance scheme and other welfare systems dealing with the unemployed and old people. The Health Service offered free treatment to the entire population along with free prescriptions, dental care and dentures. Also included were spectacles and wigs. A total of 2,751 hospitals came under the control of regional health boards. The local paper for July 10th 1948 said that to date over 53,000 residents had joined the NHS and 56 doctors were taking part. I think that this must have also included hospital doctors as I cannot imagine the town having 56 GPs. Nearly all the town's opticians had joined, as had all chemists. The participating dentists had increased from five to twelve. They certainly seemed very promising times for the nation's health.

By September 1948, I was a pupil at a grammar school. During the preceding summer I had been obliged to receive my education at Fairlight Village School; the Sussex Education Authority refused to recognise my Kent, 1946 grammar school pass. At first I felt resentful at this "downgrading", as I saw it and as a result I attracted the dislike of teachers as well as children. But as the summer passed I became happily involved and grew to love this cosy, two-room school and the Headmistress, Miss Roberts. The engaging "Miss Read" books about a village school bring her, and this long since closed establishment to mind. I felt real sadness at leaving there to go to Rye Grammar School, after having to re-sit the 11-plus exam that summer, to satisfy the authority.

The 30 minute ride to and from Rye, in a specially hired East Kent bus, played an important part in my development; it was like a mobile youth club. We, the grammar school "aristocracy", shared the bus with the pupils of Rye Secondary Modern School, who also lived in outlying villages. Rivalry inevitably existed between the two schools but I learned in later years many former adversaries crossed sides to the extent of marrying each other.
Love from Victoria.

1948

Lavender Cottage.   October 14th 1948.

Dear Marion and Beatrice,

I am so sorry that I have not written before but I have had Clar' Em'ly in bed for eight weeks with heart trouble. She is much better but does not get out of bed for long at a time. As you will understand, the housekeeping, cooking and nursing have given me enough to do but I am arrogant enough to think that I have managed very well on the whole. Kind neighbours look in to do shopping and bring books and bits for the invalid and so we get on fairly well.

I am sorry to say that James, the cat, has had a nervous breakdown. For a month he has been too frightened to come into the house and he remained out in the cold day and night. I sent him to the vet for two days but he was not any better for the change; we cannot imagine what frightened him. He was always such a cat for being nursed and petted, now he comes no nearer than the door for his meals.

I hope you are both keeping as well as possible and not working too hard. Perhaps you have the Indian summer now; I remember what a good time that was. My nursing home friend has become worse. Her niece came from New York last month and has moved her into another home but she is very miserable. Her doctor has said that she is now non compos mentis, so her house and furniture will have to be sold, not that she knows much about it. She knows only me, strange to say. It is all very sad. Please excuse my writing. My right hand is very painful and will not hold a pen properly. I am having treatment from a radiologist but it doesn't do much good.
Love to you both, Emilie.

Lavender Cottage.   October 20th 1948.

Dear Marion and Beatrice,

Your parcel was a most delicious surprise, you have sent us so much already but it was a thrill to have it. I could not resist trying the rice immediately. As I think I mentioned in my last letter, Clar'Em'ly has been laid up for just on 8 weeks so I am cook and housekeeper.

I was much intrigued to learn that a rice pudding could be made without milk, our rations have been cut again, and was delighted when it was cooked in 20 minutes; quite soft and so good. Also I sampled one of the jellies; EL is so attached to jellies but they are so poor here. Your butter is a great boon as our ration of that is cut yet again. We also appreciate the ox tongue and suet; the butcher does not send us any suet, perhaps the cows do not furnish it. The spices will add flavour to a recipe that I have found for egg-less cake.

Please forgive my short letter, the first two fingers of my right hand are so sore with arthritis it is difficult to write much. I am having radio treatment and the doctor says he will soon get rid of the pain. It's a family complaint with us; my brother had it very badly but in his time there was no such treatment.
My love to you both, Emilie.

Dear Angelique,

At last we have an explanation for a long gap in letters. I do feel for Emilie's painful hand; until I discovered the computer keyboard, arthritis in my hand made using a pen a painful experience for me too.

Although Emilie does not refer to it I must just mention that the Olympic Games were held in London in August 1948. It was a thing of wonder to me; to see the nations of the world uniting for sport instead of war. I recall seeing some of it on television but we did not own one; it must have been in the home of my parents' employers, when they were away. A lot of this sort of thing used to go on in those days; the servant playing master when he was absent.
Love from Victoria.

1948

Lavender Cottage.   October 30th 1948.

Dear Marion and Beatrice,

Your parcel of soap and accessories arrived at just the crucial moment; that morning I had contemplated the last shred of Palmolive toilet soap, somewhat ruefully. I have been economical, using kitchen soap for most things. Of course EL and CE had their share also, they were exceeding joyous! They were also pleased to have the face flannels; a thousand thanks to you.

CE is still unwell and she does not seem to be getting better very quickly. This morning she had a bad turn which scared us but she is now getting some sleep. The doctor can do little but recommend rest and he gives her a weirdly named medicine that relieves her heart.

We did enjoy Beatrice's article; she has such a knack of mingling grave and gay. The old Scottish lady was charming and we enjoyed the little bits in social security and weddings. I note you enjoy Adrian Bell; our neighbour on the left has lent CE three or four of his and she has enjoyed them muchly. I rashly took on Aldous Huxley but felt so reduced after reading one book that I gave it up. I never met anyone who was so pessimistic; he wants some lessons from you, Beatrice.

I could not find the 'heavenly blue' morning glory in our catalogue, perhaps it is under another name. Your enquiry re our corn/maize crop touched the raw! Only one seed matured but the cold snap did him in. From our church Harvest Festival they sent me two corn cobs which I cooked for five hours with no result. As they were hard and yellow I presume they were for seed only and I regret that I did not save them but it was not a corn summer anyhow. The garden is doing well; Savoy cabbages and sprouts are coming on nicely but the celery has the maggot, but with care one can find a good dishful. I tried a new kind of celery this year which needs no earthing-up but it was not a success.

No, I do not think that there are many turkeys available for this Christmas but we shall not order one anyway; £4 to £6 is a bit too much. Clar' Em'ly's niece sent her a guinea fowl last week and we all enjoyed some. It was as big as a good sized partridge and I noticed it had cost her a pound. Talking of food, (a popular subject here) the papers say that thousands of horses are being killed for meat. I had my doubts about it and I found it was like rhinoceros. Fortunately we have a cast-iron mincing machine. Fish is quite good and the cat does well.

Yes, we still have the dear old bombshell on Wednesdays and Thursdays. She has damaged quite a few bits of furniture with too-enthusiastic handling but she does actually come, never misses, even though one-eyed and weak in the knees. She never wants more money; if she does some washing for us we offer a little extra but she says: "No, that's my charge and right is right". Still I do not consider one shilling and six pence (seven and a half pence) for 90 handkerchiefs is exorbitant. She says that I wipe the floor with mine and I daresay I do, though not with those you and Beatrice sent -they are for special occasions only.

Your account of the refugees is most interesting. With you, I too am sorry that Canada is getting so many of the wrong sort but I know what hardships some of these poor souls have endured. We get some in Hastings but few come up here. We are right on the outskirts of the town, almost like country, with lovely woods around; the trees are so thick in some parts. The Ridge stands comparatively high, 500 feet, which saves us from inroads of the sea, which occasionally washes over the town proper. I must see whether I have any old photos, I used to take them before the first war but age or something made me give up my camera.

I have tried to visualise your home but can only get the idea you are surrounded by hosts of inhabitants. Sorry about my poor writing but the fingers won't work properly. I am going to the radio therapist for the last treatment on Tuesday. I must stop and get CE a cup of tea. She could not eat any dinner today owing to a feeling of sickness but I think she has had a little sleep.

Yours affectionately, Emilie.

1948

Dear Angelique,

I did like the mention of the "bombshell". As I told you, as well as being a cook, my mother did cleaning too but I don't think she ever had the destructive potential of the Lavender Cottage char; I do wish we knew her name.

Emilie and her friends were very fortunate to have such a devoted worker; one-eyed and weak kneed though she was. The war had brought about a big change in the domestic staff situation; women had found alternative, better paid work, some of them doing men's jobs and they were not keen to return to low paid, domestic service.

There is very little mention in the local paper of the refugees Emilie writes about; I did find one account of a man, described as a "victim of Nazi Germany" who had hung himself in a Hastings hotel. In the 21st century, Hastings is once again being used as a haven for refugees from another conflict.
Love from Victoria.

Lavender Cottage.   November 18th 1948.

Dear Marion and Beatrice,

Your letter telling us about the parcel you have sent is having the effect of causing great excitement all around and one does not really know how to reply; we shall certainly have a record Christmas. It is six years since we saw a turkey, prices have been prohibitive and we look forward to the advent of yours with great joy! The list of things you are sending to us is wonderful, it includes everything one could wish and will set us up for a very long time.

Our various comments will follow in due course; this is merely an acknowledgement with warmest thanks. I had to read your list of contents three times to Clar' Em'ly and the shock must have had a favourable effect on her heart, as she has been better and brighter ever since your letter came. I don't think that EL has grasped it yet but a sight of the good things will bring conviction.

Mrs Todd, the owner of the parrot, Laura, is in hospital for an operation but I am sending a message to her about the bird seed you have sent. I expect the bird will give utterance of some profane language when she sees the genuine stuff! I can report that James, the cat, is getting over his nervous attack and comes home for short stays; no doubt he will become a permanent resident when his salmon arrives.

We are all very interested in your new house and anticipate further news when all is satisfactorily settled. Forgive this short epistle; it is just pro tem till your parcel arrives.
Yours in haste, Emilie.

Footnote:-

Emilie does not mention in this letter that Princess Elizabeth gave birth to a son on November 14th. The baby was to be blessed with a long string of names, as was the custom then; Charles Phillip Arthur George, Prince of Wales. People were really happy about the new royal baby; it seemed symbolic of hope and better things ahead.

Lavender Cottage.   December 12th 1948.

Dear Marion and Beatrice,

First I must tell you that the parrot seed occasioned much joy. Mrs Todd, her owner, was still in hospital so I did not take the parcel of seed till this week because I knew she would want to be the first to present it to Laura. Mrs Todd sent over a very grateful note and is delighted but until she is strong enough for visitors I shall not hear Laura's remarks on the subject. I know that they will be, 'fluent frequent and free', to quote Bret Harte.

It was fortunate the strike did not interfere with our parcel; it all came safely and you can imagine the rejoicings of people to whom really good things have been strangers. Personally, I now feel quite unlike the

1948

housewife here, who wrote to the papers saying it was kind of the Minister of Health to send her an extra ounce of fat but it would have been even better if he had sent her something to fry in it. We can't say that now, can we?

The first things sampled were the bacon and butter and it was great to get a real slice or more of bacon. It was delicious! I took some of both into Miss Feather, the next door neighbour, (the one who does so much shopping for us) and she went nearly crazy over the bacon. You see we have been getting only one ounce per fortnight. We had chicken, mince pies and apricots next day, when Clar'Em'ly called a halt and said: 'Remember Christmas'.So now we are looking at the tinned food and hoping that the turkey will not be stolen while en route. It is ten years since we saw a turkey, the black market has got them all and we would have no chance of ever seeing one. James has not yet had his salmon; we are saving it for him. He is now more fussy than ever. The fishmonger sent him some bream last week and that cat behaved disgracefully, refusing to eat and retiring to the hot cupboard in the bathroom to sulk.

Well, it is no use trying to thank you; but the parcel has made us feel very cheery and Christmassy and anxious to pass on some of the good things that we have received. The towels are quite an asset; I always seem to be washing out tea cloths. Clar'Em'ly says that I am extravagant over soap.

December 16th   (a continuation of the same letter)

At that point, my friend in the nursing home arrived, before I expected her. She stayed until late and it was very difficult to cheer her up. Her niece, who has been here since September, has sold up her aunt's house and furniture and departed for New York. There are no other relatives; all of her old friends have died and of we two remaining, the other is over 80 and infirm. It is very sad; the only good thing is that she has plenty of money and can live comfortably.

EL takes a lot of my time as the poor dear can't write a letter except with difficulty and is very, very slow at doing anything, so she has to be helped with Christmas gifts to her numerous family and with letters too. The dear old 'blitz' has just arrived and is smashing up the bathroom and James is using language to her for shutting him in the hot cupboard, so I must away to the rescue. I am sorry to write in bits but things will come along; I suppose it is Christmas that makes people so busy.

The map has arrived and as soon as I get my afternoon rest I shall examine it as it will be interesting to see where the new house will be. Your diagram makes one realise exactly what it will be like. You say the houses have small garden plots and I shall want to hear what you grow; you know that I am keen on gardens. Poor CE has not been able to do any gardening and is not to do anymore, so her front garden looks lonesome. I have put in some bulbs and wallflowers for her but fear next year will not see the neighbours looking over the fence to say:" What a lovely garden!"

Please excuse these disjointed ramblings; it is so difficult to write with three people asking questions about food. CE sends her love and says you are dears. EL would do likewise but her head is swimming and I had better not mention correspondence.
Yours affectionately, Emilie.

Dear Angelique,

Where does the quote, "fluent frequent and free" come from and I wonder, who was Bret Harte? Laura the parrot has brought a smile to many who have read Emilie's letters; if the bird was indeed 30 years old she might well be alive today, given the longevity of parrots.

To find people who were alive during the time of Emilie's letters requires looking for those who are now in their sixties but she makes no mention of local, contemporary children or teenagers, does she? The one contact who might have helped was old Mr Scollay, who had the hardware and seed shop a few doors away from Lavender Cottage, he surely would have known her, bearing in mind Emilie's gardening enthusiasm. Sadly, old Mr Scollay died in 1999, aged 88; his two sons remember nothing of Emilie and her friends.

I did have a rewarding discovery in meeting Joyce Brewer, aged 75, who delivered milk along the Ridge during WWII, up to number 409, near to Lavender Cottage; she could tell me nothing about Emilie and her friends. However, I include a passage from Joyce's recollections because they do add contemporary colour.

Joyce wrote: - "I was a skinny-legged, fourteen-year old girl, still wearing her high school uniform, running up and down house steps, delivering milk. I wasn't old enough to drive so I sat beside the driver, an elderly ex-policeman, in an Austin 8 van and together we travelled the streets of Hastings, doing our work of national importance, keeping the families supplied with daily bottles of milk. Perhaps you have seen in collectors' shops the old, heavy, glass milk bottles that used to be sealed with cardboard tops. We delivered these bottles of milk in all weathers, seven days a week.

In those times of wartime shortages, Wellington boots were issued to Land Army Girls only, several of whom worked in local dairies. However, my boss, Mr W.E Funnell, managed to get me a pair of hobnailed boots and these were my only protection from wet feet in the rain and snow. I also wore a heavy leather coat that a customer sold to me for one pound, a lot of money then. Can you picture it? Great clodhopper boots on skinny legs under a long black leather coat; when I went clumping up and down the steps on dark and icy early mornings I must have woken up the whole street. I was never cold but I felt very tired at the end of the day after carrying that weight around." Joyce was still on that milk round until 1949. She said she always got through to her customers on the Ridge, no matter what the weather. What a pity Emilie never mentioned Joyce, with her taste for the comic she would have made much of the milk girl's wartime outfit!

You can see that the pending arrival of the turkey was an important event in the life of the Lavender Cottage ladies. So important that at one time I considered re-naming this book," Thank You for the Turkey" but bearing in mind the modern connotations of the word turkey I thought this title could go against me!

We have to wait till early January to hear more of the turkey. My family, happily established on the farm, enjoyed a Christmas dinner of a big, plump chicken and double cream with our plum pudding. I was

growing as plump as that bird, living on the unaccustomed luxury of home made butter and new laid eggs. We were never cold, we had a plentiful supply of logs from the surrounding woodland and I was well clad in the cast-off clothing of the teenage daughter of my parents' employers. For us, many aspects of austerity were already over, but not for others.
Love from Victoria.

Lavender Cottage.   January 3rd 1949.

Dear Marion and Beatrice,

I am sure you will be amused to know the excitement there was over the turkey. Its pending arrival has been a source of great interest to our neighbours too. Even the post man has been asking daily, "Has it come?" All expressed sorrow when the answer was negative. On Christmas day we resigned hope and our invited guest had to partake of common mutton. However, with the help of your gorgeous mincemeat and fruit we managed very well and our guest said that she enjoyed her meal.

And then IT came! It was a beautiful turkey and we spent Saturday in trying to find a dish large enough to cook it in and on Sunday we persuaded it to go into EL's larger oven, even then there was not room to baste it. A wonderful bird; it melted in the mouth! Clar' Em'ly is tearing her hair over what the turkey and the postage must have cost you. EL's vegetarianism went by the board and we and the neighbours are enjoying every scrap.

A letter came from the Air Mail people to ask if it had arrived undamaged. If so, no reply was needed. I did not answer but was tempted to do so and say what a lovely bird it was. I need not tell you how we are enjoying the other good things that you sent to us. My friends rejoiced over the dried and tinned fruit. I go for the bacon; breakfast is a joy with the lovely frizzly juice to sit over. We are hoarding the pudding and other things, except, of course, the butter and fats. We gave some to the kind old lady over the road as we like to share our good fortune.

I want to take the little crippled man a piece of turkey; he is such a patient fellow and always in pain, poor lad. Our neighbour, Miss Feather, who thinks you are wonderful, received a parcel from Yorkshire and her silly relative included a packet of Persil washing powder that burst and spoilt most of the contents. Laura, the parrot, is having a rollicking time with her seed and her owner gave us some eggs out of gratitude. Dear me! You will be tired of all this food talk.

I must add that James, contrary to his usual likings and dis-likings, has taken to turkey in a scandalous manner. He must recognise the difference between that and chicken; we had one some time back but he declined to touch it. He has, of late, reformed his habits and comes in early now. Maybe the salmon attracts him though he does not eat much at a time. However, that is not material; I can easily dispose of it.

I do hope you had a nice time at Christmas; we were very quiet. On Boxing Day I went to see my friend in the nursing home. She was unaware it was Christmas time and only after a long chat did she know me. I hope I shall hear further of your new home in due course.
Yours affectionately, Emilie.

Lavender Cottage.   January 25th 1949

Dear Marion and Beatrice,

I am feeling very bad about not replying earlier to your letter of the 9th inst, in which you tell me of 'Cousin' Beatrice's illness. Most stupidly I retired to bed on the 5th with a nasty attack of flu, nothing like Beatrice's or Cousin Ethel's, but disagreeable enough to confine me until this morning and I fear my letter will not be very intelligent; flu seems to leave a most owlish feeling behind.Like you, I am not sorry we are in January, though we can't grumble at the weather very much. It is certainly chilly but the sun has given us a very good innings and the sunsets have been beautiful.

1949

The worst aspect of after Christmas is that churches and institutions insist upon issuing reports and accounts and such like unpleasant things at this period. CE has just wound up a fourteen year church treasurer-ship, owing to her health, and I am trying to evolve something fresh for her reports. One is for a convalescent home and the patron is a countess but if you saw her you would conclude that the charlady had volunteered to act in that capacity. The poor old dear is over 80 and one can't hear a word she says, but still, a countess is a countess, even in Socialist England.

My other report is for our little church and that is easy because no one minds what I say and everyone is pleased and a good tea comes along to compensate for the statistics. Ours is a humble little church and we have no special service for Christmas. Our minister went along to my friend's nursing home on Christmas Eve and gave a nice service with some carols afterwards.

We are now looking forward to a piece of real bacon for breakfast; I can hear Clar' Em'ly wrestling with the tin. I went in to assist but was informed I was as much use as James (the cat) at that job so I retired as gracefully as possible. James has dispensed with one tin of salmon; I fear his uncultivated taste prefers cod but when that is off, he condescends to a richer diet.

EL's sister and her husband have flown to the Argentine to see their son, poor little EL misses them. She can not write to them herself because of her poor head but she allowed me to send an epistle for her. We all send our love and warmest wishes for a Happy New Year. I hope Beatrice will behave herself and not indulge in any more illnesses. I am glad Cousin Ethel is better, she is a wonder! This paper is not an extravagance. A friend of CE sent the note paper to her but as her letters are short and to the point it would be useless to her.
With love to you both, Emilie.

1949

Dear Angelique,

This letter is written on headed notepaper, a great luxury for these austere times. Typically, Emilie makes the best of a turkey-less Christmas but didn't they all enjoy it when it came? What is "frizzly" juice? Perhaps she means the fat and juices from the bacon; anyhow, I love the word!

Miss Feather, who crops up a number of times in the letters, lived at "Claremont" 406, The Ridge, so she was Emilie's immediate neighbour. Until 1947, Miss Feather had shared the house with her father, the Rev. James Feather, a Methodist minister. We must presume he died not long after as her name alone appears on the subsequent street directory.

The countess is emerging in the letters as quite a personality, isn't she? She was a very significant, local benefactor and you will hear more of her later. Isn't it odd how Emilie, so out of character, denigrates this elderly patroness? At least we learn that she is not impressed with titles. I found a delightful story of another Hastings benefactor in a January 1949 edition of the local paper. An obituary revealed that an unknown person, who had been a "Father Christmas" to the poor families of Ore Village, situated where The Ridge ends, was a Mr W H Langdon. For 25 years he had sent anonymous gifts of coal, meat, fruit, vegetables and groceries to these families, who never came to know who the donor was. Mr Langdon's agent in the good deeds was the local Welfare officer, appropriately called Mr A E Christmas, whose work brought cases of need to his attention. This had gone on throughout the war, with rabbit being substituted for scarce meat.

Perhaps the spirit of Christmas still prevailed when the local food control authorities decided not to open official enquiries, when it was discovered there had been irregularities in the Hastings School Meals Service and Civic Restaurants. But some matters would be followed up, such as the illicit making of cakes by kitchen staff at the Mount Pleasant Centre. I know this news item sounds very Alice in Wonderland, Angelique, you may well smile at it, but most transgressions of the food control regulations were taken very seriously!

1949

Family butchers were still having a testing time. At a meeting of the Hastings and St Leonards District Meat Traders Association, the Hon Sec, Councillor A J Oliver, said that in every other trade things were looking up but all the butchers could look forward to was maintaining the 1/- (5p) per week meat ration. There was a general dissatisfaction with the quotas of offal, one butcher complained that he had been given only two ox livers to share between 500 customers.

There was probably much to tell about Edith and her family but for the most part, she remains an almost shadowy figure in the Lavender Cottage household; sometimes, it seems to me, that her status is rather like that of James the cat, a pampered pet.
Love from Victoria,

Lavender Cottage.   February 12th 1949.

Dear Marion and Beatrice,

I fear that my last letter, written on a Sunday, would not reach you quickly as there were no stamps in the house that I could steal and it was foolish to post it without. Anyway, I wanted to send you a note to tell you that we had the BACON and oh, it WAS bacon! I took a piece into my neighbour and she visited us this morning to tell us how much she had enjoyed it. You see, we are allowed only two rashers a week each and as the pigs get almost starved nowadays the bacon they provide is fit only for the birds, after we have struggled with it. It really is awful to keep thinking about food but it is a general topic of conversation whenever people meet.

I am having a brisk time, still writing reports and invitations for our two annual meetings: I will be glad when they are both over. CE is busy making a cake with some of the dried fruit you kindly sent. The cake is to go to her niece, a nice girl who is a domestic science teacher way down in Gloucestershire. She works up until 9.00pm and has no time to make cakes for herself so it will be a real godsend. EL is devouring an orange and James is going round Clar' Em'ly's legs, hoping for some more fish, which he won't get.

EL and I went down town this morning and brought him home a perfect whale of a fish, a fair portion of which he has demolished already. My nursing home friend came to tea on Thursday. She has developed an enormous appetite; she polished off 2 large mince pies, (your mincemeat) 2 thick slices of bread, butter and jam, 5 substantial biscuits and some sweets. I like seeing people eat, don't you? The nursing home gives her no teas to speak of so I don't wonder she gets hungry. It's not right to comment on her appetite but food is all she seems to look forward to; very hard luck on her, poor girl.

The sunset seen from The Ridge is gorgeous; the sky is a brilliant orange-red behind the oak and fir trees and I have to break off writing to look at it now and again.
I hope you are all better and we expect news of your removals later on.
We all send our love and James would join in if he only knew.
Yours affectionately, Emilie
(This letter ends with a tiny ink drawing of a fat, seated cat with enormous whiskers)

Lavender Cottage.   March 11th 1949.

Dear Marion and Beatrice,

I expect you are in the throes of moving and hope it is not too arduous a job. We shall be interested to hear of your progress. By the way we have not the new address but I expect that this will reach you anyhow.

I am glad to report that the various meetings are over for the present. I am a bit tired of writing minutes and reports. The countess duly attended and presided over the meeting at the convalescent home and was as inaudible as usual but her presence assured us a notice in the local paper. I cannot say it was a lively meeting; I had prepared a little speech, intended to be comic, but the treasurer squashed me! Poor man, the finances were so gloomy that he was quite depressed.

You see, the home has not been "taken over" by the government, otherwise it could be maintained by the helpless taxpayers, upon whom the burden of the hospitals and institutions falls nowadays.

Here, we are going on as usual with nothing exciting, except a chimney on fire, yesterday, while I was out visiting my nursing home friend. Poor Clar' Em'ly was pretty scared but the kindly next door neighbour rushed in and smothered the fire with earth. Later the electric sweeper came and finished the good work. James nearly had a fit while the machine operated; he is a nervous animal and also a very fussy one.

CE has been eating much porridge of late and has a special kind, which James also appreciates. Lately, this has not been obtainable and she got a substitute, of which she did not approve. "Anyway", says she, "It will do for James". Would it? The little beggar would not look at it and in the end the charlady removed the packet. The former brand has now come back and James is happy, he enjoys his nightly porridge again.

Before I forget, I wrote to Cousin Ethel before Christmas and have recently had my letter returned," not known" I must get a new address book; my old one is so scored and crossed it is illegible and it is a wonder anyone gets the correct epistle.

Talking of writing, I re-read one of Beatrice's articles the other day and wondered why she didn't try to write a book; there is a market for good literature now, especially that of a pleasing nature. Think it over!

I dropped in to see Laura the parrot the other day and was greeted with "Ain't yer got a 'ome? Damn yer eyes!" I thought this impolite, where do parrots learn these remarks? His mistress is quite a refined woman but..., she has nephews!
Yours affectionately, Emilie

Dear Angelique,

I am using the local newspaper archives extensively for background material to Emilie's letters. Studying these large, leather-bound tomes is hard work. The Hastings and St Leonards Observer was a broadsheet in Emilie's day and when fifty-two of these albeit, austerity-sized copies are bound together, they are as big and heavy as an oak, coffee table-top.

Grappling them to the research table is not the end of the problem. As I am short, the huge, rigid book presents quite a challenge. In order to read the top-of the-page items, I alternately stand, kneel on the uncomfortable plastic chair or sprawl across the table, trying, meanwhile, to make notes. I do hope you enjoy my hard won little morsels of contemporary news.

One of these items reported in 1949 was that Hastings had a larger proportion of old folk than any where else in the country. Many could not make ends meet, although 40% were eligible for some kind of non-contributory pension, which they had never claimed. In Hastings there were then, as now, many nursing homes for the elderly and with no system of inspection in place then, one can imagine the conditions in some of them.

At first sight, the list of things Emilie's visiting nursing home friend ate for her tea make amusing reading, until you think how hungry the poor soul must have been. I fear this was not just rationing but possibly parsimony on the part of the nursing home owners. When a member of my family was a nurse in one of these establishments, in the affluent 70s, she was expected to make a 7 ounce tin of salmon serve as sandwich filling for 14 patients and that was the full extent of their supper! I hope that nearly thirty years on, elderly ladies have become more out-spoken about their requirements.

We now begin to get intimations in these letters of the problems that will dominate Emilie's final years, in her reference to" finding rooms", after Edith has gone. But then Emilie brushes these anxieties aside in the recounting of humorous domestic trivia; she uses anecdotes about a chimney fire, a fastidious cat and a profane parrot to make light of what must have been a difficult and worrying time.

After the 11th March letter there are none till August; Edith's deteriorating health and Clar' Em' ly's indisposition kept Emilie busy.

1949

During this period two forms of rationing ended. On March 15th clothes rationing was stopped; this had been in force since 1941. The utility scheme, in which garments were made under a cloth quota system, continued and clothing price controls stayed.

The other items to be de-rationed were chocolates and sweets. The nation went mad on buying confectionary and within days sweet shop shelves were bare. In Hastings, there was a family confectioner called Maynards, who made their own wine gums; the wartime version, probably low on sugar and flavouring, were not very inviting. Proof of this came during the post rationing, sweetie-famine when there were still plentiful supplies of Maynard's Wine Gums in their shops but nothing else! Sweet rationing was re-instated on July 14th.
Love from Victoria,

Lavender Cottage.   August 9th 1949.

Dear Marion and Beatrice,

It was kind of you to write while you were on holiday and send each of us a card. I hope you will have a real good time; you must have wanted a rest after all that moving. Cousin Ethel kindly sent me your new address some days back but I couldn't get any letters written as EL and CE have been very poorly and there seemed such a lot to do.

Clare is rather better now but poor little Edith's head is very bad, though she can get about and eats well. It is sad to hear her try to tell you something when it is almost impossible to interpret it. The doctor can do nothing for her now but give her bromide; he thinks she may have a stroke sometime. Personally, I think she has had one already. My nursing home friend is no better; she can talk but has no memory at all.

James is bright and consumes a large quantity of fish but he will not come indoors, even at night, preferring to fight the neighbour's cat! The drought has burnt up nearly all our garden produce; I never saw such a summer! I try to keep the vegetables well watered so as to provide for the winter. This weather is good for the holiday people anyway.

Please excuse this dreary letter. Have a real good holiday. I am posting the Strand Magazine today.
Much love,Emilie.

Lavender Cottage.   September 28th 1949

Dear Marion and Beatrice,

I have had a marvellous communication from the Midland Bank here and we could not understand it at first. Clar' Em'ly said: "You get a taxi and go and find out what it means". I obeyed, taking my identity card as requested and saw a very nice man who told me that the Toronto Bank had forwarded some money to me.

When he presented me with it I was struck silly and enquired the name of the sender. After an interval he found it and it was yours! I had suspected this but the Toronto puzzled me. My dear, how more than good of you, and such a sum too! I can't thank you enough. It came just as we were feeling a bit worried about our future arrangements, when poor Edith Lake goes and the difficulty we may have in finding rooms. It cheered us up no end.

Of course, she may go on like this for a long time, the doctor cannot say but it is so cheering to have money to fall back on isn't it? This is only a hurried note of very, very many thanks to you. I will write again but with Edith roaming around and wanting attention all day it is hard to get a moment for a decent letter and I wanted you to know as soon as possible. My love to you and CE's as well. James would join us too if he knew but he has just had a nasty five days at the vet's and is very cross.
With very much love, Emilie

1949

Dear Angelique,

Poor Emilie, how weary she must have been! It was such a hot summer and she was over 78 years old and she had two invalids to care for, one very confused. Apart from the casual help of the destructive 'Blitz', she had every other household thing to do, including care for the garden; no wonder the letters were not written. It does sound as if Edith had experienced a stroke as Emilie suspects; with all her invalid friends she seemed to be very well informed in these matters.

In July there had been an announcement that the NHS was costing more than had been expected; 2/6 (12 p) a week per head, not the 1/4 (7p) first calculated. Not that this concerned the Lavender Cottage ladies as we gather they were all still private patients; I fear this was engineered by their doctor for reasons of his own.

During the heat wave of 1949, the sinking of a new dairy well on the farm where I lived had caused ours in the garden to run dry, so a new source of water for us had to be found. The local water diviner water was sent for and it was discovered during larking about that I could divine water.

With the necessary forked hazel twig in my hands I walked about until, as I passed over a hidden flow of water, the stick would twist violently. My family suspected that I was creating the phenomenon myself and so, Ron, the younger of my two older brothers, living with us after his demob' from the RAF, grasped my hands, as the twigs writhed in response to running water. So tight was his hold on my hands the bark on the twigs peeled off; that little stick would not stay still, it felt like a snake! They were convinced.

More interesting to me than this, was the arrival of German ex-prisoners of war, to work on the farm. The youngest, Irwin, was 22, very Hitler Youth and arrogant. He still wore his uniform cap and sneered at us for the English peasants he thought us to be. The oldest was Karl, 38, an ex-officer and seasoned solder of many WWII battles. In perfect English he would talk for hours about the war to my father and brother and good friendships were forged.

Together, during that hot summer, the English and German men built a concrete road across a field to Peter James Lane and Karl showed himself to be not only hardworking but also amazingly inventive in the face of shortage of materials. Karl was engaged to an English girl from the village; they took me out to Hastings to tea one day. The whole thing made me wonder what the war, ended only four years previously, could have been all about. That road, built by former enemies in the summer of 1949, stayed solid for many years.

In August I saw the film "Hamlet", with Laurence Olivier; to be able to buy the book of the film I gathered and sold sacks of early apples for 1/- (5p) each that month, to raise the 21/- (£1.05p) needed. I still have that hard-won book.

As a seaside resort, Hastings had a splendid season. The beach and promenade were thronged with visitors. The crowds were so thick it was risky to take your eyes off a child for fear of them being lost. The weather certainly was good for holiday people, as Emilie said but Hastings still bore the terrible scars of enemy bombing, with ugly gaps in rows of buildings while others, in a dangerous condition, were shored up with gallows-like timber scaffolding.
Love from Victoria.

Lavender Cottage.   October 17th 1949

My Dear Marion and Beatrice,

I know that you will be sorry to hear that Edith Lake passed away on the 9th inst: As I said in my last letter, she had become very incoherent and her head grew worse. We had to get in a nurse for her at nights and later for all day. The end was very sudden. She was unconscious for 4 days and never spoke again, just going peacefully. It was for the best but we miss her terribly.

We have hardly grasped yet how this will affect us materially but I will not say anything of that, as I know little of the family's arrangements but I expect we will have to leave Lavender Cottage. However, that would not be very soon, I think.

I want to thank you again for your most kind and generous gift, it was most good of you and at this time it will be especially a great help. I have not answered your letter referring to this but I will let you know more later on as to what is happening.

I am just going to start another batch of letters received from friends and relatives of Edith, who all appear to have written to us, instead of to the family. Please forgive a short epistle for the present. My love and good wishes for the new home and renewed thanks for all your thought and kindness.

With very much love, Emilie

Dear Angelique,

Here, the sad news, which had been expected; the death of Edith Lake. I found a fragment of her death notice in a local family history record, dated 27.10.49, it said: Lake Edith. Widow of William John Lake of Gravesend, late of Brighton. Whatever extended family she had clearly regarded Emilie and Clare as her nearest and dearest by the way they responded with letters of condolence to them.

In a later letter we learn that Edith was buried at Charing in Kent, which is a pretty village, 40 miles from Hastings. We do not know the date of burial but the weather for the period when the funeral took place may well have been appalling. In Hastings it was the wettest week since records began in 1875; there was torrential rain and squalls that reached 60 miles an hour; tremendous seas flooded the town centre.

Emergency food was delivered to flood-trapped families, which was organised by the School Meals Sub-committee; I do hope it was not investigated by the Food Control Committee at a later date! At five hundred feet above sea level Lavender Cottage was safe from the floods but no doubt they felt the full force of the rain and the 60 mile

1949

per hour winds. So sad to read of the uncertainty that has come into the settled life at Lavender Cottage-I feel I want to rush in and help them, don't you?
Love from Victoria.

Lavender Cottage.   1st November 1949.

Dear Marion and Beatrice,

We don't know how to thank you for the gorgeous parcel, which followed your letters very rapidly. Clar'Em'ly and I spent a most happy hour rejoicing over the contents. Everything is so nice and helpful that it is difficult to differentiate. You see, the meat we get here is very poor and CE is happy to make pies that we can really enjoy with your meat. The bacon you sent is a great treat; we had to cancel the order at our little shop as what they sold was tough and fatless. We opened the tin you sent at once and had some lovely sandwiches. We are also going to surprise a neighbour with some. I was so glad to see the tea as I am a tea drinker but we usually give some of ours to a little crippled man.

Our only regret is that little Edith will not be able to share, open the parcel addressed to her nor have any of the butter; the ration is so scanty now. The things you mention as coming later sound so Christmassy; raisins, nuts etc, will be a great treat. We haven't seen any this year except at exorbitant prices. We did not make any Christmas puddings this year as Edith's illness kept us so occupied. I know that turkeys are very expensive and it seems wicked to ask for one but that which came last year was lovely.

Mrs Todd, owner of Laura, the parrot, will rejoice in the seed and so will that rapacious bird. Mrs T. gives us eggs when her hens are laying, so it will be a pleasure to take the packet of seed to her. I hope you will excuse this awful scrawl; the weather has turned so cold and my fingers are stiff. I am also rushing because I want to catch the postman to avoid delay in posting to you. He comes at nine o'clock and will post anything for us.

We feel very lonely since Edith went; it was very sudden at the end. I do not know what will happen as this house was not ours and is to be sold. The executors are quite willing for us to stay on if possible; Edith left us half the purchase money so I hope we can arrange not to move on, as other houses are impossible and lodgings prohibitive. However, I feel that something will be arranged. I will let you know what happens but probate is not yet passed and it will probably be some months before anything is done.

Yours affectionately, Emilie.

PS. James is very well

Dear Angelique,

There is no doubt that the Canadian parcels are still very much appreciated. Although it was more than four years since the war ended, the austerity period continued. In September the milk ration had been cut twice, from three pints per person per week to two and a half; a week later it was cut yet again to two pints per week. In October the price of petrol was increased by two and a half pence to 2/3 (12p) per gallon.

A recipe section in the local paper explained how to extend the meagre ration of bacon by using it as a filling for jacket potatoes and you could, "add an egg if you could get one". The Hastings and St Leonards Observer published a letter of thanks, addressed to the local people, who had kindly supplied old stockings to the Royal East Sussex Hospital for use in the plaster bandaging department. Think of the uproar such a measure would cause today!

Love from Victoria

Lavender Cottage.   November 16th 1949.

Dear Marion and Beatrice,

I had a most wonderful surprise today. A letter came from a bank in Hastings asking me to call upon them and bring my identity card. I can tell you I was all excitement and rushed off as soon as I could get away from doing the chores. Imagine my feelings when the cashier smiled on me because he had remembered me. He said; "I am instructed by the Bank of Toronto to hand you the sum of £32 pounds". Oh dear! I was so excited I forgot how many shillings there are to the pound.

Anyway, I tore home to Clar Em'ly, who was waiting to learn why the bank had wanted me. Well, of course we knew who had sent the money and we both felt how more than kind it was.

It came when we were feeling rather sad over Edith's going and wondering a little what was going to happen to the house; your great kindness cheered us up no end and we began to take a brighter view of things, which I think will not be so bad after all. The executors are very kind and will do all they can and anyway, nothing can be settled until after probate has been passed, which will probably not be until June next.

So here we stay in the meantime and I hope it will be as long as we live. People are so kind. Why you should be so good to us I don't know but you may be sure I appreciate it tremendously and Clar'Em'ly wants to thank you too; she thinks you are wonderful-so you are and she has been very good in helping me too. I can't say all I wish as the nursing home friend is coming to tea and the post goes at four.

Yours affectionately, Emilie.

PS You see the money came so soon after the other amount that I could not believe it! Excuse confused letter but I must get it to the post before the invalid arrives; she does stay so late.

Dear Angelique,

Aren't those Canadian girls just the kindest of people? I feel sure if they had been able to take a hand in Emilie's and Clare's legal and accommodation affairs there would have been a much more agreeable arrangement made for them , but more of that later. But such a gift; £32 was a great deal of money in 1949.

1949

I have not told you much about Marion and Beatrice; Wendy Johnson told me that Marion worked in an income tax office in London, Ontario. She was very good with figures and managing money, well organized and very interested in family history. Of course, we know how generous she was to Emilie; she was to many others as well. Wendy gave me a couple of photos of Marion that look to be about 1950's; she has an attractive face and a warm, open smile.

Beatrice was the women's editor of the London Free Press as well as drama critic at the Grand Theatre in London Ontario and the Stratford Festival in Ontario. She wrote a column for the Free Press and also poetry and had a book of poems published called White Winds of Dawn. She died in 1979 of Alzheimer's or something similar.
Wouldn't they both have loved to have known that Cousin Emilie's letters are now the subject of a book?
Love from Victoria

Lavender Cottage.   November 28th 1949.

Dear Marion and Beatrice,

We really are so overwhelmed by the two parcels which have arrived, one on the heels of the other. We are delighted with all the different and interesting things; I had not tried any of those jolly little tins with all kinds of sweetmeats in them. I suppose they did not exist when we were in Canada. The only thing I remember regarding food in those days is Oysters, removed from their shells, at an exceedingly reasonable price. I do not recall such nice things as those you send.

It is not easy to express preferences and it sounds invidious, if that's the right word, but the bacon is first class, so unlike our tough little rashers. We are hoarding your tins of bacon for the use of ourselves and our neighbour. Clar'Em'ly told me to say thanks for the nuts and that we will not have to make a pudding now for this year. There are so many little things to be sampled from the parcel but I shall have to wait a while. I tried some lovely sweet stuff yesterday-I can't tell you the name at present. I am in bed, trying to get rid of a fiendish cold in the head and cannot go downstairs to refresh my memory.

I must mention the bird seed. Mrs Todd, the parrot's missus, said that Laura received the first instalment with the polite remark, 'Damn yer eyes!' and began to weigh in with great appreciation. Scandalous bird! She must have lived some time at sea. James is well and comparatively polite though he always insist on the most comfortable chair.

We should have liked to hear Beatrice's speech. I do envy her as I can't say anything unless it is written. I was to have given a paper on Thursday but the minister has just rung up and told me to stop in bed.

I hope the little girl is better. I wonder why a red-headed doll? It seems the child might be artistic but this is only a guess. I keep your letters to enable me to reply on another occasion; no doubt I have left out everything I wanted to say.
Much love from Emilie

Dear Angelique,

The little girl Emilie mentioned was the six year-old Wendy Johnson, the source of these letters; she had just had her appendix removed. Wendy denies she grew up to be artistic and says, "I consider people who devise something from nothing to be artistic. I can follow knitting patterns, crochet patterns, love to cross-stitch and now do quilting, but these are patterns artistic people have come up with and I'm just carrying them out". Later, on reflection she added, "Actually, I have been artistic once or twice in my life. I wrote a Christmas poem, a short one, which my Mom set to music and it's on her CD. My one claim to fame"! She sounds as self-effacing as Emilie, doesn't she?

Re parrot! Even just the mere mention of Laura, the parrot makes me smile, in fact the mention of any parrot; possibly thanks to Monty Python! They seem such bold, matey birds, no wonder sailors liked them. A young friend of mine has a parrot that has meticulously picked out all of its feathers, apart from those on its head. The vet has diagnosed the bird as being depressed and has prescribed

tranquillisers. Poor naked creature; it looks like an oven ready chicken! Perhaps a good, Laura-style swearing session would do it good; release all those birdy tensions! See, now you are smiling!
Love from Victoria,

Lavender Cottage.   November 21st 1949.

 Dear Marion and Beatrice,

Your letter about the turkey has just arrived. Please forgive my brevity, I have just come through a week in bed with the flu and feel very thick-headed. The prospect of a turkey is wonderful. CE says the 5th or 6th of December would be best for delivery as it should keep in the cold weather. We have already issued an invitation for Christmas dinner.

We have not invited James as he is not attached to birds, unless they come into the garden for their daily meal! This week he has insisted on sleeping on my sick bed and occupying the middle so it was not over comfortable for me but he was a happy cat. This is not a letter but just my answer to your question about the turkey.
Yours in haste, Emilie

Lavender Cottage.   December 13th 1949.

Dear Marion and Beatrice,

We are in a perfect whirl, surrounded by good things for Christmas. Two parcels arrived a day or two back and this morning the postman appeared with a sturdy box about which he was most curious. He is a nice old man and takes great interest in our correspondence. He guessed wrongly and left without knowing it was the piece de resistance, if one may call it that; THE TURKEY!

It is a lovely bird, so plump and good looking; the excitement overpowers me and I can foresee a delicious dinner with carefully chosen tit bits to give to the next door neighbour and to the old lady opposite. She will have a dreary Christmas as she is encumbered with a somewhat disagreeable invalid, who is bed-ridden, hence we can't invite them to dinner.

I gloat over the Christmas cake and others, too, shall sample it. To Clar'Em'ly it is pleasing too but her practical mind rejoices most in butter, cheese and bacon. But the dried fruit is a great joy to her; she can make buns, etc: now. By the way, I tried some of the Tea Bisk yesterday and evolved some quite good scones. But we have not tried half of the good things yet so we must report later on. CE keeps telling me, "this will be handy or I must try that", so I get quite muddled but am enjoying the anticipation exceedingly. I will let you know how her experiments turn out.

CE has just called from the bedroom where she is having a rest to ask me to tell you how much she liked the sugar cane. I never knew she liked sweet things but she says that this is different.

We are trying to get a man from the town to take James' photo. It is difficult as they are all so busy just now. But we would like you to see him as he is now 16 and may not last for long. However, his appetite is remarkable and there are no signs of it fading just yet.

We do miss EL so much. How pleased she would have been with the parcels, the sweet things especially. It will seem a strange Christmas without her. We both send our love and warmest thanks for all your kindness. You really are too good and spoil us utterly.

Yours affectionately, Emilie

Dear Angelique,

It sounds like a magnificent turkey and parcel and, typically, Emilie lists a collection of neighbours to have a share of the goodies. I have been thinking about the frequent mention of neighbours and wonder in which houses they may have lived. Records tell us that Mrs A Todd, the parrot lady, lived at 433, The Ridge. A Herbert Watson ran the Ridge Grocery Stores and William Rowe had a newsagent's shop, both just a few houses away from Lavender Cottage.

Since Emilie's time, many old places have been demolished and new houses built on the site. There still remains, opposite Lavender Cottage a very old, stone, one-level dwelling with a tipsy roof; it may have been a lodge gatehouse, very picturesque. I can find nothing of its history. Close by, there was a grand family residence, Sandrock Hall, built in a romantic, turreted style, by a German I think; it eventually became a convent. It is now divided into luxury flats and there are costly new houses in the convent gardens. In the same stretch of land there was a vast, gloomy, Victorian guest house called Netherwood, 379, The Ridge. This place was home for the last two years of his life to the controversial Aleister Crowley, a famously reviled man, who meddled with the occult and indulged in shocking and well publicised sexual perversions. He died December 1947. What an unlikely neighbour for the innocent Lavender Cottage ladies!
Love from Victoria

Lavender Cottage.   December 20th 1949

My Dear People,

You must excuse my delirious letter as I am in a whirl and so is Clar' Em'ly. We have had such a rapid flow of lovely parcels that we don't know quite where we are. In fact, I could not now name the exact days upon which they arrived. When I told the postman that the first parcel he had delivered had contained no less than a turkey he smacked his lips and said, "Ah, you don't see much of them nowadays". He is really too old to be tramping round with letters and CE and I decided that he should taste the turkey.

Then he returned with another parcel which turned out to contain a gorgeous quantity of soap. Again, we rejoiced, having heard on all sides that that soap is scarce in Hastings and this kind is certainly scarce. I know you won't mind but one or two folks are delighting in pieces. One friend was really joyous at getting a piece of Palmolive, her favourite. Clar' Em'ly, being practical, gloated over the Lux Soap Flakes and I did so appreciate the dainty products.

On another day, your letter came telling us that an additional turkey was on the way; on the same afternoon it arrived. My dears, wasn't one enough?! This one was hardly liftable but both are noble birds. The first is already with the butcher, a new man, as we had to give up the other, owing to the poor quality of his meat. Our new butcher has the turkey in his 'frig' as he calls it and the other will go to him to keep until after Christmas. He is a funny man. He said; "I 'as me doubts about them there gibs (giblets?), but if they seem to be goin'orf I'll bring 'em back so's you can cook 'em". He will get a shock when he sees the second bird. As with the soap, we will share some of the turkey with others. I am sure you will approve.

Well, we can't thank you adequately. CE says that tears come to her eyes because you are so kind. She wants to send a piece of turkey to her brother-in-law, who came over from Hurst Green-18 miles away, this morning. His wife, who is very delicate, lives on slops and his two daughters are vegetarians, so poor George doesn't get much chance between them. He says that he will have to get a chicken for himself so we decided he must have a piece of turkey.

At that point our church minister came in to have a chat and we were so glad because we had just packed a few things from Canada in a box for him to take to his wife. They are such nice people and not over well off. We are anxious to send you a book but not knowing your tastes, it is difficult to select; would you be kind enough to let us know? The bookshops here have such strange products now; too many sex problems and other undesirable stuff.
With our united love and thanks and EL would join if she were here.

Yours affectionately, Emilie

1949

Dear Angelique,

Emilie usually starts her letters with Dear Marion and Beatrice, doesn't she? Here she seems so overcome with excitement and gratitude that only "My Dear People" seems to suit the occasion! The way she writes about the butcher he sounds straight out of an Ealing Studios comedy, or is it that those 50/60 years old film depictions of trade's people are perfectly accurate? Speaking of films, an item in the national press in November 1949 claimed that television was taking over from cinema; not in Hastings it wasn't, certainly not in Lavender Cottage nor our house. Hastings and St Leonards still had seven cinemas in 1949 and in my family, wireless held sway. The picture of families gathering round the wireless then, as they do with TV now, is no myth.

The nation was very sad at the start of 1949 when British comedian Tommy Handley died. His radio show, with its familiar and loved characters, catch phrases and quick fire repartee was a big favourite during and after the war. Hitler seemed less frightening to me when Tommy dubbed him Herr Schikelgruber. I cannot think Tommy Handley was Lavender Cottage listening. There, I imagine, it was classical music concerts, talks, news and current affairs.

My family and I sometimes used to take the infrequent, country bus from Fairlight to go into Hastings to see a film; the last bus back home was 10:20pm. We often saw the final moments of films whilst standing at the back of the cinema, with coats on, poised to run to the seafront bus stop. I experienced my first visits to the theatre in Hastings during the summer of 1949. My parents took me to see the Court Players in the little theatre on Hastings Pier; I think it was "Charlie's Aunt". We had also gone to The White Rock Pavilion, as it was called then, and had seen Clarkson Rose's summer variety show, "Twinkle"; heady stuff for a coming 15 year-old.

I smiled at Emilie's comment about "bookshops having strange products, too many sex problems and other undesirable stuff" I wonder what it was she spotted; in those days women's magazines were about matching hats and shoes, knitting patterns and no sex before marriage!

1949

At 12:00 am, December 31st 1949, Derrick, the eldest of my two older brothers, not long out of the Royal Navy, had his first child, a son and my parent's first grandchild. It did not occur to me till midnight 1999 that he was truly a half century baby; what a fiftieth birthday he must have had! Brave Emilie kept her sense of humour and kindness through all her troubles in 1949, how I wish I had known her!
Love from Victoria

1950

Lavender Cottage.   January 5th 1950

Dear Both,

Will you be good enough to forgive my typing this? My right-hand
fingers are all rheumatics and decline to hold a pen straight. It is this
cold weather and they will improve in time. I want to tell you how very
much we enjoyed the turkies, (by the way, I think my spelling is wrong
and it ought to be turkeys, but you can't expect good spelling when
you are writing of those delicious birds). In fact, we are still enjoying
them for we did not cook them all at once. Our next door neighbour,
who comes from Yorkshire, said that she had never tasted such birds.
The old lady with the bed-ridden invalid of over 90 were both thrilled
at what I carried over; other recipients were equally enthusiastic.

I think that the fowls over here don't get much food nowadays; those
one sees in the shops look as if their diets had been remarkably
meagre. The cranberry sauce was a great feature as no one seems to
have sampled it here for years. It is hardly possible to mention every
good thing that you sent, but the bacon, butter and cheese are simply
great and have also been enjoyed by others. We haven't really got
down to everything yet and CE says I am not to eat all of the sweet
things at once but to keep them for a rainy day. We keep thinking how
EL would have enjoyed all this but perhaps she knows all about us.
The parcels have been a great comfort to us. You will perhaps smile at
that but when one's future is uncertain you can't help feeling worried,
and it is nice to sit down to a good dinner of nice things.

The probate on Edith's will has not yet been passed but in any case the
house must be sold. We know she did not mean that to happen as she
said we could have it for our lives but unfortunately that was not put
in the will. Someone may buy the house and let us remain, as tenants.
We have until March, so something may turn up. I feel very optimistic
but Clar'Em'ly is not over well and it bothers her. We are both
bordering on 80 years and it would be trying to be turned out after 20
years of living here, but one can but hope for the best.

I am sorry the typewriter goes rather crooked but the little thing is
about 40 years old. I must take it to get it repaired, when there is a
chance of getting it done within six months. We shall be very glad to

1950

have news of you, when you have time; to hear what sort of Christmas you had and how the new house is going and if Beatrice has written any more articles. Please tell us what kind of books we can send. Clare keeps asking me, when am I going down town to get one, which I want to, only it is a bit risky to choose one. The modern writers are a bit peculiar; rather like our James, whose age seems to be telling on him, for his temper is not at all what it was.

The parrot's mother renews her thanks to you every time I see her. Laura eats all her seed now but uses awful language; I think it is her way of expressing her pleasure, what a funny way of showing it! We both send our greetings to you and hope the New Year will be a happy one in every way. I will let you have any fresh news that comes along. Yours affectionately, Emilie

Dear Angelique,

I can just imagine you saying, 'Oh no!' when you read the words about Edith not having put into her will instructions about Emilie and Clare remaining in Lavender Cottage. Edith must have bought the house when it was first built; I understand that was in 1930; Emilie's reference to a twenty year residence backs this up.

Ahead of the forthcoming February 1950 election, the local paper announced that its size was being increased to 10 pages; paper was still severely rationed but there was an extra allocation of newsprint for the election. It was a three cornered fight in Hastings and the candidates were: Cooper -Key, Conservative, Cohen, Labour and Hurd, Liberal; at that time Hastings was a traditionally Conservative constituency.

As Emilie is still writing about food matters, a news item about a flourishing, home produced source of food is appropriate. 'Backyard farmers' were producing 25% of the nation's eggs and their rabbits supplied 30,000 cwt of meat per year. This item is from a reported meeting of the Hastings and St Leonards District Poultry and Rabbit Club. The chairman, Mr L A Eldridge said that they were 'doing a wonderful job in helping the nation along'. He was therefore angry

1950

that the White Rock Pavilion management had refused permission for a rabbit show to be held in their lower hall because "rabbits are smelly". The management later relented.

It is interesting to note that in Germany, food rationing ended on January 16th 1950. In Britain, The Ministry of Food continued to publish regular bulletins in the national and local press, to inform people of the fluctuating values of the points in their ration books; no wonder people used to say that Britain won the war but lost the victory.

My family was fortunate to have dairy farm supplies and my father and brother, as agricultural workers, got extra rations. There was no need for us to keep backyard rabbits; the fields were full of them. How I hated to see my father come home, gun over his elbow, with a handful of furry, blood-soaked little corpses. My mother did the gutting and skinning. Yuk! To me now it would be like eating James!
Love from Victoria.

Lavender Cottage.   January 30th 1950.

My Dear Both,

 I can't typewrite this as my machine is so trying, so you must excuse the writing.
We have been having some delightful meals recently. Excuse the mention of food but it really is important nowadays. Clar' Em'ly says we are living like fighting cocks; I don't know how they feed but if they do as well as us, they are lucky! I sent the minister's wife a lump of Christmas cake and she rang up next day to say that she was eating it all day long. I haven't heard yet of any ill effects! Then a guest turned up here for tea yesterday and he enjoyed it too. So we go on, something new every day. The nuts are a rare treat and we go sparingly with them as they seem scarce over here.

Before I forget, I am to tell you that The Strand magazine is being discontinued in March as it does not pay. I have ransacked the public library to find a substitute but so far without success. I will send a few specimens but they are not so good.

1950

As you see, we are still here. The probate has just been passed and the executors came in here to take EL's things away. It seemed horrid to see all her things go, things that she prized specially. They are going to sell this house and we are hoping that the buyer will let us stay on as it is practically impossible to find a place to here. There are 12,000 people in Hastings looking for houses or flats. We certainly don't want to move or leave the town, so we go on hoping that the purchaser will be obliging.

The time of institutional meetings has arrived once more and I have been grousing over annual reports. I expect you know what a secretary's job is like. The old countess writes to say she will attend if weather permits. I trust it won't permit as she is quite inaudible. However, even in nationalised England, a peeress can attract. My other annual meeting is for the church and it is quite jolly. I guess Clar' Em'ly will make cakes for the tea from your Crisco . She cannot do much with the synthetic lard, poor soul. Aren't the housewives grumbling about it? There was a column in the newspaper about the margarine, lard and fats in general.

Folks are very busy about the coming election and there is a great deal of uncertainty as to how the votes will go. A good many say they will not vote at all but I think that is a mistake. Of course, it is trying to have three sets of people competing, as we have in Hastings, especially if you feel sympathetic with two of them. It seems so absurd not to have proportional representation, doesn't it? Our new neighbour will not vote at all but we shall both go to the poll. We listen to the speakers on the wireless very conscientiously; they all promise so much and will probably do so little.

Well, I mustn't talk politics, especially when CE is doing accounts. It is so distracting, especially when she is a pound out! I expect the pound will come to her in the night, it usually does; she is the most careful housekeeper. Oh dear! I wish I could write like Beatrice. I was reading one of her articles the other day and envied her the easy flow of the language it contained. When is she going to write a book? We have read one or two American books lately, at least CE has, and she says that they are much better than English novels nowadays. I am not reading any at present, being occupied with meetings and trying to write a paper for our Literary Society.

We both send very much love to you both and hope you are not being frozen. It is hard for us to keep warm at present. The birds eat nearly a loaf a day, poor things but James is fatter than ever!
Love from Emilie.

Dear Angelique,

There's so much to comment on in this letter. As Emilie keeps mentioning the Strand, a magazine I vaguely remember, I did a bit of research on it. The Strand was the first and possibly the best of the popular illustrated monthly magazines; it was founded in 1890 and was aimed at a mass market. It was cheaper and more readable than the literary monthlies of the time and had many illustrations.

Despite the expense, it aimed to have a picture on every page, at a time when the arts of photography and process engraving were in their infancy. Costing sixpence, the Strand was half the price of the existing monthly magazines. It also featured stories, such as Sherlock Holmes by Arthur Conan Doyle. The publisher, Newnes, deliberately aimed for the middle classes, and the magazine projected an image of that class in print. It was said that its readers included Queen Victoria; the Strand was regarded by foreigners as the epitome of Englishness. So now we understand why Emilie, with her middle-class background, patriotism and love of reading regarded the Strand so highly and wanted to send it to her cousin and friend in Canada.

In spite of what Emilie said, there was a good turnout in Hastings for the 1950 election, especially when compared with today's figures. Voters from the Royal East Sussex Hospital made their way to polling stations on crutches, one old folks home had an 86% turnout and taxis did a good trade with eager voters. One of the town's leading confectioners, Henry King and Fiest, played it safe with a celebratory cake for each party displayed in his shop window. Predictably, the Conservative candidate, Cooper Key, won and also increased his majority from 3,597 to 12,432; the count took place in Hastings Pier

Pavilion, often the scene of civic ceremonies those days.

At my school, Rye Grammar, a week before the General Election, we held mock elections and I stood as the Labour candidate. I became a socialist zealot but my fifteen and a half year old eloquence was as nothing in confrontation with the victorious, sixth form, good-looking male Conservative candidate. I think he benefited considerably from the female vote! It snowed for Election Day, 23rd February, so heavily, that getting about was difficult. I waded over snow-clad fields to find a neighbour who could drive my parents to a polling station to register their Labour vote; if I could not win a school election I was doing my utmost to make sure Labour won the General Election. They did, by a whisker. Winston Churchill said that Parliament would be in an unstable condition; Labour had a final majority of six.

How painful for Emilie and Clare to have to stand by and watch Edith's belongings taken away. The task of disposing of the deceased's things is so wrenching but to have strangers come into their shared home to do it must have been almost like having the bailiffs in. Emilie's comments on the prospects of finding a house were justified. The lack of housing in Hastings in 1950 was severe. During the war, 439 houses in the borough were destroyed or left totally uninhabitable by bombing, and a further 14,818 properties were damaged. A proposed council plan to build social housing during the fifties was not yet underway but Emilie and Clare would not have qualified for this scheme; these homes were designated for young families and there was a long waiting list.

I have been sidetracked down a very interesting research avenue by Emilie's mentions of the countess. With the help of a local museum and historical society I learned a fair bit about her. I am sure Emilie could not have known much about Lady Brassey or she would not have been so dismissive of her; she was very much in Emilie's mould. More of the countess in 1951.
Love from Victoria.

1950

Lavender Cottage.   March 15th.1950.

Dear Marion and Beatrice,

A few days ago I sent off a book to you that we hope you will like; it seems quite varied. There went with it a little book on the various places about here but unfortunately the map stopped short of our district, which you will see is a little distance from the sea.The final Strand has gone today. I am sorry its publication has ended as I cannot find any magazine as good. I am sending you two others but they are not nearly so good. We are still enjoying some of the Christmas things; we are not nearly through the list. I hoard the cheese for occasions also the soap, which seems too good to use.

The main news is that the house is sold and the new people are letting us stay on. They are turning the house into two flats and we will keep nearly all the part we have had so far. CE is a bit reduced in spirits because she will have a microscopic kitchen instead of the one she has now. She complains that she will not be able to swing a kitten in it, let alone James! Talking of James, we could not find a man in the town who would come here to take a photograph of him so our neighbour went down to town to buy some films and took them for us. As James objected strongly I am very doubtful of the result.

We held the meeting I mentioned to you in my last letter and the countess presided; she was attended by a nurse and was in a bath chair, which arrived attached to her car. She was quite inaudible, as usual, but it really didn't matter and the local paper gave us a notice with the emphasis on the name of Lady Brassey. I'm glad that is over for a year! I wonder what you thought of the election here; it was an odd one and nobody seemed satisfied. Hastings is ultra Conservative and the result is always certain. We gave the Liberal our votes but knew it was a forlorn hope; he was such a nice young man.

Talking of cats, which I wasn't, how is yours? I was reminded of him by glancing at James, who has taken my chair and buried his face in his white toes and gone to sleep.
I'm afraid I haven't any special news. I will write again when all is settled.
With love from Emilie.

Lavender Cottage.   March 24th 1950.

Dear Marion and Beatrice,

Herewith the snaps taken by our neighbour one morning when our hair
and dress were untidy!   We thought you would like to see them.
Unfortunately, the sun is in James' eyes and he could not open them
properly. However, it is like him. I also enclose an extract of the
speeches at the Guildhall which may interest you.
We both send you much love and hope you are not being frozen. It is
very cold here at present. We have just had a lovely tin of meat (yours)
for dinner.
Yours affectionately, Emilie.

Lavender Cottage.   April 1st 1950

My Dear Marion and Beatrice,

The ham arrived safely last evening; it is a glorious one and had a
lovely flavour. It was put on to cook at once and today we enjoyed a
luxurious dinner, our neighbour also partook and said it was delicious.
The bacon we get is so tough and has to be stewed for hours to make
it tender but James does enjoy the juice, so we have been buying it. But
now we are countermanding it for some time. Our very best thanks for
a great treat.

I have no fresh news to give you at present; we have got as far as
signing the lease for our half of the house, so I expect things will begin
to move shortly. They say it will take three months to do the
alterations. In the meantime, we are trying to find room for pieces of
our furniture that cannot be squeezed into our future, smaller living
space, while also endeavouring to find time to get the garden tidy, so
as to do some planting. I find the landlord does not seem to take any
interest in the garden.

I hope you won't find the Sussex Anthology too boring. I still cannot
find anything in the way of magazines as good as The Strand. Most

magazines seem to be made up of instructions regarding clothes, which make very dreary reading. I expect you will be amused at the photographs I sent. Everyone says Clar'Em'ly looks so stern but I think it is very like her. We both send much love and I will let you know when any fresh news comes.

With love from Emilie,

Dear Angelique

I was delighted when Wendy Johnson sent me copies of the photographs that Emilie wrote about in the previous two letters. Wendy said that these had turned up quite by chance and I found the discovery as exciting as she did. At last, a face to put to the letters! Emilie has a merry, puckish face, with high cheek bones and, indeed, Clare does look stern, as they stand arm in arm, in the open front door of Lavender cottage. The dearly loved and squinting James looks just right on the door step.

The Hastings and St Leonards Observer carried a report of the Catherine House AGM, which took place on 7th March. Miss Emilie Crane, Hon: Sec: announced another year of progress and said that 200 ladies had been received at the home in 1949 and there had been more Christmas guests than any year since before the war. Thanks were given to Dr Anne Beattie, the home's physician and these were renewed by the chairman, Mrs B. Muller who added that, 'we cannot be thankful enough to Dr Anne'.

Patrick Joy, Hon Treasurer said that St Catherine's had spent £305 on repairs and £1,005 on furniture but £13,720 still remained in various funds, (were they too well off to be 'taken over', as Emilie described it?) The meeting closed with thanks to Lady Brassey.

There had been changes to our household on the farm. The 'gentleman farmer' for whom my parents worked, decided he needed more live-in workers; he put a caravan in a field for their accommodation and my mother was to give them three meals a day in our home. One of these workers, who appeared at our family meal table, was a 22 year-old, ex-Royal Navy man, who was part of a government, demobbed servicemen's agricultural training scheme. He was gentle, reserved, good looking, had excellent manners and treated my mother with courteous respect. Of course, I lost my heart at once, what romantically inclined, nearly sixteen year-old wouldn't? After a while he asked my parents if they would allow me to go for a ride on his motor bike.

During this time, when my young life was burgeoning, Emilie's was falling apart. Signing the lease for half of the house was a hasty step and I wonder if there was some kind of pressure. And yet, Emilie's sense of humour and optimism prevail; at this point in her life I do wish she had been less sweet and trusting.
Love from Victoria.

Lavender Cottage.   April 18th 1950.

Our Dear Cousin Beatrice,

Thank you so much for your Easter card and letter-a lovely thought. Of course, this epistle is to you both but as we received yours last it was only right to address this to you. Clar'Em'ly says please call her Clare as the other is too frivolous; she is much stimulated by having new cousins.

I am writing this in the midst of bangs and crashes. Six men are pulling the house to pieces and converting it into two flats. A new staircase is going up and our bathroom is to be a small kitchen and a bath will be put upstairs for us. Our present kitchen will be a hall and the landlord's stairs. Our linen cupboard has gone and the linen is at present distributed all over the house. We can't find a cup or plate; in fact I never saw such an upheaval. Clare says it would be easier to move house but that would be impossible as thousands in Hastings are looking for homes and prices are prohibitive now. At least we will keep a bit of garden. The garden and greenhouse are in a poor state as no gardener comes now. A nice young man has put in a few vegetables for us. The new landlord and his wife care only for flowers and fruit

Miss Emilie Crane, writer of the letters, on the doorstep of Lavender Cottage with the beloved cat, James.

Emilie with her friend and Lavender Cottage companion, Miss Clare Marriott

Lavender Cottage, The Ridge, as it was in June 1950.

Lavender Cottage, September 2001.

Miss Marion Ellis, of London, Ontario, Canada sent generous food parcels to the Lavender Cottage household during and after World War II.

Beatrice Taylor, Marion's friend and Emilie's "adopted cousin", was the Women's Editor of the London Free Press in London, Ontario, Canada.

The Ridge, near Beauport Park. Winter, 1947. "Trees were coated with ice, birds died by the thousand". Picture source: Les Englefield.

The Ridge, Winter, 1947. "The weight of the ice brought down telephone poles and wires into the hedges". Picture source: Les Englefield

Miss Phoebe Hows. In her youth she nursed
Florence Nightingale and was Emilie Crane's friend.
Picture source: Hastings and St. Leonards Observer

Lady Idina, Vicountess Hythe
and Countess Brassey. The
Countess sat with Emilie on the
committe of a "Home for
Retired Gentlewomen". Picture
source: Bexhill Museum.

Hastings Town Centre floods, mid-1940s. The flags round the Albert Memorial suggest a celebration of some kind.
Picture source: unknown

Bombed Out. 1943. The Ore Village shopping community that served The Ridge. Picture source: Hayward Family

James is the only unperturbed occupant here. He is most intrigued by the alterations and rejoices to get under up-heaved floorboards. The workmen keep asking us to remove him as they are afraid he will get lost. James found the new staircase last night and went down to the landlord's rooms, in the new part of the house, the doors of which I had carefully locked. I have had to shut James in my bedroom, the only undisturbed place, but he is quite happy on my eiderdown with a hot water bottle; the noise does not seem to disturb him at least .We reckon we shall get straight in about two months.

Meanwhile, one's social duties are getting neglected but fortunately, it is a slack season with the church and convalescent home. My nursing home friend has also been neglected but I shall be able to make up time shortly. We are finding great solace in the supplies from Canada, they make such a difference. So much here is synthetic; the soap you sent is most refreshing. I have just had to use some of the first aid things you sent as I foolishly upset a kettle of boiling water on my legs last night while filling hot water bottles so I am going about swathed in bandages.

The new budget came out yesterday and has much upset people here who have cars; 9d (4p) a gallon extra is rather stiff. There was a slight, very slight, decrease in income tax but coffee is to be increased. The housewives refused to buy fish this week owing to ridiculous increases in price, but not James' fish; generally speaking, the prices of goods bear no relation to their value. Please excuse this rambling letter; the workmen's noise is very disturbing but the men are nice and trouble us as little as possible.

Yours affectionately, Emilie

1950

Lavender Cottage.   June 7th 1950.

My Dear Cousins,

I make no excuse for sending you the enclosed poem. I thought it would give you an idea of our front garden in the spring days. The beauty is passing now but it really was a blaze of colour, so I had to break into verse. It is not a summer garden and it will be poor this year, as drought is killing all aspirations on the part of seedlings; I fear we are to have another summer without rain. I hope you are more fortunate.

It would be interesting to hear about your garden, I am very keen on growing things and am in a worried state just now as I am confined to bed with a funny head. I keep wondering whether our occasional gardener knows the proper procedure as regards plants. Of course, I am sure he does not. I know he cannot dig a proper trench for the celery nor give the onions some fertilizer nor weed the carrots etc. Clare says that I worry quite unnecessarily. Anyway, something will come up, even if it's only weeds, which I call very unsatisfactory and is of no comfort to me!

I have just had dinner, which concluded with some of your delicious pineapple. Next week we reckon to open a tin of bacon, it's so different from what one buys. The soap and Maple Leaf Soap Flakes are so good and last a long time. You will see how we are well up in useful things. This is a short letter; the banging from the workmen that goes on all day, is disconcerting and does not add to any intelligence I possess. Still, the alterations will be over by next week, I believe. Our love to you both and we hope that the Winnipeg floods did not come too near; the account was horrible. I am sorry that this village doesn't supply sixpenny stamps; one has to go to the town for these. The best of all from us both,
Yours affectionately, Emilie

COLOUR.

I think this patch of cottage soil
Has trapped a rainbow in its toil:
Such opulence of riotous hue
Will hardly let the earth show through,
A mount of purple, topaz-crowned
By saffron alyssum and round
The red flame gilly flowers upstart
To kiss narcissus' golden heart,
While prodigally the rock cress spreads
White stars upon its emerald beds.
From tulips' rich-dyed sunspot bowls
A gush of Orient splendour rolls;
Forget-me-not in sapphire mist
Enwraps viola's amethyst:
From lilac flags, as in a well,
Glances the pink of asphodel.
Beyond, that ferny screen lets by
Quick flashes of a bluebell sky,
While all above the branches hold
Their riches of laburnum gold,
And may bloom bounds on every side
This little patch so glorified.

Dear Angelique,

I felt sorry for the two elderly ladies, as they suffered their house and life being turned upside down. Of course James would enjoy the disruption; it gave him a chance to explore all those out of reach places that had been denied him before. I acquired a visiting cat today; the sudden arrival of spring enabled me to leave the door to the garden open and a black, only just out of kitten-hood, cat keeps wandering in and inspecting every corner of the house. His green velvet collar bears the name George, another pussy with a chap's name.

Recently, Wendy sent me a copy of the photograph of the exterior of Lavender Cottage. It was more rustic looking in 1950, with plant trellis round the doors and windows and flower borders right up to the house, not plain walls and an asphalted drive, as now. The extensions and conversions to the property cannot be seen from the front of the cottage. Mrs Smith, the present owner of the extension, expanded in the 70s and now named Pilgrim Cottage, allowed me to visit her late last summer; her part of the house was never occupied by Emilie and Clare. Its upper landing ends with a blank wall, where it joins Lavender Cottage. The larger part of the garden has been retained for Pilgrim Cottage and while Mrs Smith, a keen gardener, showed me round it, I felt the spirit of Emilie and could imagine her pottering about there. Even as late as the 1950s The Ridge was still more like a country lane, with very little traffic. Now, an almost non-stop flow of vehicles makes trying to cross the road on the Lavender Cottage bend a risky business.

Whitsun 1950 brought the first public holiday without petrol rationing but also an increase of 9d (4p) a gallon in April, plus a further increase in June, the price of petrol was 3/- (15p) per gallon, the highest since 1920. August brought 45,000 visitors to Hastings and special trains had to be laid on. Soap rationing ended but that does not mean to say there was much available and what there was poor quality.

My friendship with our new farm worker, John, flourished. He invited me, with my mother, to go to the White Rock Theatre to see the Hastleons, a local, fund raising amateur dramatic group, still very active today. They performed Noel Coward's, 'Bitter Sweet'; Coward said that he hated the operetta but I thought it made a perfect evening; a melodramatic plot, sentimental tunes and at my side, a wonderful fellow, discreetly holding my hand! He also took me for a few excursions on his motor bike; I was leading an odd double life, schoolgirl and girlfriend at once, an unusual situation in those days. Love from Victoria

1950

Lavender Cottage.   August 26th 1950.

My Dear Marion and Beatrice,

I am so sorry I could not write earlier but very stupidly, an attack of blood pressure took hold of me and the arbitrary doctor said: "Go to bed and stay there". So obediently, I stayed there for four weeks. Poor Clare had a brisk time and I don't know how she managed but she said; "If things have to be done, the strength to do them is given".

I do hope you are both keeping well and that you are enjoying a holiday. Possibly you have better weather than is bestowed upon us. This month has been bad with storms and rain and one feels sorry for the holiday makers, especially those with children. The boarding houses have a trick of packing people out of doors after breakfast and refusing to allow them to return until evening, so the poor souls have to flock to the cinemas most of the time. These are the times we are thankful for the peace of Lavender Cottage and garden. I regret to say that James has not been behaving well all this summer. He has stayed out all night and if brought in he rushes out of the house as if it were haunted. It is very strange and we think he must be ill, though his appetite certainly contradicts this assumption.

The landlord and his wife are nice people but our interests are very different in character so that conversation is difficult. However, things might have been much worse and a house move would have been trying, even if we could have found a place within our means. I am wondering if the periodicals we have sent you are of any use. I am so sorry The Strand is no more; it is difficult to replace it but there was talk of it starting again. I send Everybody's magazine, because of the King's life being in it, which may interest you. We send love to you both and hope to have a line later on.

Yours, Emilie and Clare

(Also James, although he seems to be hors de combat just now)

Dear Angelique,

No wonder Emilie has blood pressure, with all the stress and upheaval she has endured during the spring and summer; and she did smoke. Not that it was regarded as particularly harmful at that time. In fact during the war people were encouraged to smoke, 'good for the nerves' they said.

I could not find anything about Everybody's magazine on the internet so I turned to friend Ivor White, retired press photographer, for help. He said, "I have only a vague recollection of the "Everybody's" format, but I think it was popular with the working class for its many competitions, short stories, recipes, readers' letters, crossword puzzles and an agony aunt. My dad used to bring it home, and sometimes sent for mail order items, like a Swiss Army Knife, or a John Bull Printing Outfit." No wonder Emilie is uncertain about Everybody's suitability; it sounds a bit removed from The Strand but it was very popular; a favourite waiting-room read, along with Punch.

A famous visitor to the town in September 1950 was Anuerin Bevan, father of the National Health Service. He spoke at the White Rock Pavilion, saying, 'It would be a fundamental departure from the basic principles of the scheme if it was ever found necessary to charge for the National Health Service'. I do not remember the bad weather of August 1950 Emilie writes about, in retrospect, every day seems sunny to me.
Love from Victoria.

Lavender Cottage.   October 3rd 1950.

Dear Marion and Beatrice,

Two glorious parcels have arrived and we have had a most exciting time unpacking them. You are such kind and wonderful people and seem to know what will be most needed and appreciated. The "meaty" things will be a great treat; Clare is very ingenious but even she finds it difficult to make much from corned beef or an attenuated bone. Our poor animals seem to be on a perpetual Lenten diet. Our rations of bacon and butter have been cut again and the sugar supply has been too limited for much jam-making, so you may imagine how pleasing it is to look forward to making a little parsnip wine. Well, I know you both object to too many thanks but really all the things are just lovely and cheer us up tremendously.

The weather here is also bad but I hope you will have a good and fine holiday. I was very interested to hear you would go to Montreal. I remember that city so well, except that I can't remember where we stayed only that a hill, where lovely flowers could be gathered, was almost opposite to the house. I can visualise a picturesque cathedral where I went to services at times. Otherwise, it was not a happy time as my mother had her stroke there and was an invalid for years, until she died. The other places you mention I do not know, being profoundly ignorant of America. My only recollection is that of eating a lunch of cold chicken, after crossing a river in a small boat to the New York Side, being accompanied by a young man rather deficient in intellect, who lost our lunch basket on the way back to Guelph. I fear my memory retains most of the cold chicken and little of Niagara Falls.

James is not very well and has had a visit from the vet, resulting in an extracted tooth and some unpleasant medicine to which James objects strongly. I hope your cat is behaving otherwise. Anyway, I hope you will have a very enjoyable holiday, do take care of yourselves and don't climb too many mountains, if such there be in the parts you are visiting.

Much love to yourselves, Emilie

Clare wished to add a line so I must leave a little space:

Clare writes: -

My Dear Both,

I'm simply delighted with the parcel you so very kindly sent me, it was good of you. We have already opened one of the tins and found it excellent. Two invalid neighbours have also come in for a bit; they think you are such nice people, our opinion exactly.

Much love to you both dears.

Clare Marriott, Cousin by Adoption

1950

Dear Angelique,

This is the only time, as far as we know, that Clare has put pen to paper for Canada. Her writing is small and neat, unlike Emilie's round, flowery style; how tidy the Lavender Cottage household account books must have been. It's interesting to have some references to Emilie's time in Canada. This is the only mention of a male companion and he does not sound very pre-possessing, does he? But then, as she confesses to remembering the cold chicken better than the Falls perhaps he is being done an injustice.

In 1950 butchers thought that they were the most put upon retailers during the period of austerity. During their October, Hastings trade conference they sent a resolution to the Minister of Food declaring: "It is impossible for a butcher to make a fair profit on the present retail price of meat". They also claimed that they were being forced to sell B class meat to their customers at "A" class prices. The axe fell once again on the supplies of newsprint and it was back to austerity sized newspapers. In matters of food, my family continued to be cocooned from austerity, many country people were, even throughout the war, but we were not very well off for money. Most of my clothing was hand-me-downs; even my grammar school uniform was a miscellany of a few regulation items but mostly recycled cast offs. My obligatory, brown felt school hat was, in truth, a ladies hat from the 1940s. I hated it. To protect myself from the derision of other pupils I rolled and bent it so that eventually it looked like a tramp's headgear. My feeling was that if I was obliged to wear a freak hat then let's all have a good laugh. My hat became famous! And, of course, out of school I was the girl friend of somebody special, so, who cared? My parents became concerned about the effect of my double life on my education and general well-being and put a total ban on my relationship with John. He, being a gentleman, honoured this. I, being a savage, did not and cried, argued and became so generally devastated that weekend contact was eventually permitted. Already a maverick, my dislike of the restrictions of school life grew. I must have been awful, my poor parents!
Love from Victoria

1950

Lavender Cottage. October 13th 1950.

Dear Marion and Beatrice,

Your letter has just arrived; everything you sent us is so good and acceptable that it is difficult to differentiate but I will do my best, since you have kindly asked. I will put the items, (pretty large "items"), in order of preference. The butter, tinned bacon, dried milk, sultanas and raisins are invaluable. We only get one egg and two rashers a week each, of inferior quality, and butcher's meat lasts only three days out of seven. Christmas puddings are scarce but we can usually manage to get one.

The fat you send is always totally different from the synthetic lard we get which has to be grated. The pastry and cake powders we can buy here and we are well off for spices. We did mange to get a pound of sultanas and raisins and generally we can get dates. Today, we had a pie made from one of your tins of hot-pot, it was real good. Even James approved. It is joyful to think of a turkey, we are already issuing invitations on the strength of it. I think that drawn, (gutted) would be best.

The sugar is most welcome as it has been "cut" again but we are quite well off for it at present as a friend also gave us some she had from Barbados; as soon as the parsnips come in I shall make some wine. There are so many things in the parcel that are useful but I think we have given you a long enough list. It is strange that the North Country people are so well provided in every way but I don't suppose they are as lucky in having such friends as you abroad.

This is a scrappy letter but we thought it advisable to write at once in view of what you said so I won't stop to comment on your holiday at present.

Yours affectionately, Emilie

1950

Lavender Cottage.   October 28th 1950

Dear Marion and Beatrice,

The packet of soap arrived quite safely and indeed is a boon; I am afraid we use a good deal as our old char is not exactly economical but she does not see well, so it is excusable. We have also been indulging in extra butter and have enjoyed the chicken immensely. James does enjoy the gravy that comes forth; he is so old that we feel we must indulge him.

We are glad that you can read The Everybody's, though we keep looking for something nearer the quality of The Strand. Just now the printers are hard put to it, owing to a strike. Some of the papers and magazines are reduced very much and the Radio Times has vanished altogether, so that we get no details of performances. It does not affect us very much though Clare is always on the lookout for a Beethoven night. The country is in a state of unrest just now, as I expect all countries are. Every one I run into asks: "Do you think we shall have another war?" All one can say is: "I hope not." What do you think of Truman? Personally, I have a good amount of faith in him. Our landlord and his wife have a television set and they invited us to see it but we found the white glare too much for our eyes, so have not repeated the experiment; though we rather wanted to see the ceremony at the new House of Commons. I have put a description of this into Everybody's but the papers seem to take a long time to reach you.

The weather has decided to be icy; ground frosts are frequent visitors and gardening is almost impossible. Clare insisted on going out yesterday to plant some bulbs and paid for it by having a bad night and continual cramp. So instead of going to church tomorrow I shall finish that job myself. She is very proud of her bulbs and if the moles don't get them there should be a fine show. We both send love and many thanks to you and hope you are not feeling the cold too much. I remember hanging out the washing at Guelph on an apparatus like a Catherine Wheel. It was dry but my, it was chilly!
With love from Emilie.

1950

Dear Angelique,

What war is this you may ask, to which Emilie refers so anxiously? Some call it the forgotten war, because, for many, the memories of it have been overtaken by the Vietnam War. The Korean War lasted from June 1950 to July 1954 and was triggered by North Korea invading the southern, independent half of this divided nation. How strange that this conflict is mostly remembered now by the TV show M*A*S*H; a comedic and sardonic look at a battlefield medical station.

So, Emilie and Clare got to see television at last and obviously did not think much of it. Perhaps reception was poor on The Ridge but in any event, the black and white picture often tended to be full of glare or blurred and people had to sit in darkened rooms to watch it. My parents did not get a TV set until 1959 and yes, you guessed, it was a hand-me-down!
Love from Victoria

Lavender Cottage.   November 9th 1950.

Dear Marion and Beatrice,

I keep wondering whether I have written to thank you for the lovely lot of soap; generally I put down what letters I write in my diary but there seems to be no note of this. Clare says that I didn't write and she may be correct. If that is so, it is strange but you must kindly put it down to another attack of blood pressure. Anyway, the parcel is worthy of many thank you letters. Nice soap is most welcome as it is not easy to come by; we are enjoying it every time; even James likes the scent! The poor boy has just had a visit from the vet and his mouth was pulled about and his teeth inspected. He is now over 16 and I fear we shall not keep him much longer, though his appetite never fails, which is a blessing. At the moment he is sitting on my coat purring, having got over the ruthless, though kind handling.

Clare says you will understand our appreciation of the meat, among other things, when I tell you that the local paper is advertising horse meat at the butchers. We have never tasted this and it may be all right but somehow it doesn't sound attractive. This past week has been chiefly occupied by war news, which is nasty, also the death of Bernard Shaw; a wonderful man that. Opinions differ very much, he was either liked exceedingly or thoroughly hated. I am in the first class as he was so fond of animals.

Love from Emilie.

Dear Angelique,

The horsemeat Emilie mentions put in an appearance in our home. My father enjoyed it but I did not like the yellow fat and strongly flavoured meat; besides, Dolly and Polly, the farm's two cart horses were my friends. How could one consider eating their like? A very famous vegetarian passed with the death of George Bernard Shaw; in one obituary he was described as a scandalous genius who had subversive opinions, wore strange clothes and lived on vegetables. It added that he wrote plays that nobody understood, he claimed to be better than Shakespeare and left money to establish a phonetic alphabet. The obituary did not make mention of his fondness for animals.

Hastings had a splendid November 5th Guy Fawkes' celebration in 1950 with bands, crowds, a procession, 250 flaming torches, a monster Guy, music from a van and fireworks. The event was also used as recruiting drive for the Special Constabulary, Fire Service, Hospital Service Reserve and Civil Defence, there was clearly no thought of disbanding the latter with the threat of war from Korea.

Was it blood pressure which had afflicted poor Emilie or could it have been an undiagnosed stroke? But, as ever, she is more concerned with James than herself, he is becoming a very costly invalid.

Love from Victoria.

1950

Lavender Cottage.　　　December 19th 1950.

Dear Marion and Beatrice,

Clare and I are in a state of daze! We have just been undoing the parcels, which have all arrived safely and the contents are overwhelming! CE almost shed tears, which does not sound cheerful but you will understand. The things are marvellous; everything is just what we wanted and our Christmas visitors will have a good time. We just feel we are fortunate above our deserts to have such kind folk and our thanks will be going out to you all the time. Mrs Todd, the owner of Laura the parrot, was very excited about the seed and the bird expressed great satisfaction with remarks I cannot quote, but damns and blasts were numerous!

I have had some sad duties this week; my nursing home friend passed away Saturday last and she is to be taken to the crematorium next Saturday. Her niece has been cabled for in New York but it has fallen to me to swear that cremation was desired, as there was nothing of it mentioned in the will.

Forgive this depressing interlude but I wanted to tell you the reason for my haste to write; please excuse the handwriting. We send you both our warmest love and thanks. I will write again later. We hope your Christmas will be a very, very happy one.
Much love from Emilie

1950

Lavender Cottage.   December 26th. 1950

Dear Marion and Beatrice,

I have been trying to write to you before but it has been a bad time; what with my friend's death and having to obtain a permit for cremation, also to attend the funeral which meant a journey to the place where her sister is buried. Unfortunately, my late friend's only relatives are in America and there are no other great friends over here, except a very old lady, who could not attend.

The turkey was a gorgeous sight; so white, large and plump. He refused to go into our baking oven so I had to borrow our neighbour's, which the bird so filled there was no room for basting. However, he turned out beautifully; we had never tasted a finer nor more delicious bird. This morning I have been going round taking some portions to people who could not run to turkey and there is still heaps left for ourselves and others. The cranberry sauce goes so well with it and there was ample in the way of accompaniments for a good finale to the Christmas dinner.

Of course, we have not yet fathomed the depths of the good things in your parcel, but Clare, (the housewife!) wishes to speak her rejoicing at the sight of butter, bacon etc. James, of course, appreciates the salmon most of all; no interest at all in the turkey. Funny things, cats! How nice of you to send the cards; now that wasn't necessary, was it? We are still trying to find a substitute magazine to send you and hope to do so soon. I cannot get down to the town, the cold has restricted one's journeys but a change is foretold and I hope for better weather. I hope your trip has been a successful one and that the coming year will be of the best for you. Both of us send you much love and happy thoughts, and not only when we sit down to a meal!
Yours affectionately, Emilie.

1950

Dear Angelique,

Although 1950 has not been an easy year for Emilie, she is still doing things to help and bring happiness to others; she is just under two months off her 80th birthday.

Hastings Council proposed that in preparation for the next year's Festival of Britain, floodlighting would be set up to illuminate the White Rock Pavilion and White Rock Gardens, Warrior Square, Alexandra Park and Hastings Castle. The Hastings' hotels and guest houses were ready for a big influx of holiday visitors and the town, according to the local paper headlines, looked forward to a "Gay Christmas".

The war in Korea continued to dominate the news and at the end of the year there was an element of the anxiety of Christmas 1939 in some families; there were those who wondered if there might be a general call up in the New Year but others regarded the whole thing as being so far away that it had nothing at all to do with Britain and they enjoyed the festive season. I had been longing for a particular pair of grey and white fur gloves as a Christmas present; they arrived on Christmas Day, given to me by John; they had cost 19/6, (95p) nearly a third of his week's wages.
Love from Victoria

1951

Lavender Cottage.   January 18th 1951

 Dear Marion and Beatrice,

It seems a very long time since I wrote; I have been trying to send you a letter since Christmas. One cause for delay was that I couldn't get down to town on account of the weather and the local shop is devoid of both air letters and stamps for long intervals. It sounds silly but it is a bit awkward up here, especially when we have snow, as they never sweep it away. Our neighbours, Miss Feather, the old lady and her invalid and the parrot's mother have all shared in the parcels you sent; I fear that they don't get much in the way of presents. I must tell you how useful the handkerchiefs have been to me. I had a fearful cold after my friend's funeral and as our charlady has been laid up for a month with bronchitis she could not do any washing, so it would have been so inconvenient without hankies.

The government have cut the meat ration again down to one shilling (5 pence) per person per week. We did not mind that too much as we had your parcels but we do feel a bit annoyed at coal being reduced to one hundredweight per household per week; we burn almost 5 hundredweight in that time. However, we can get logs; I fear that many poor people do not have these. As Clar'Em'ly says; 'We are very fortunate.' Even James is well fed as his fish ration is quite good and I cannot see that he has lost any weight. He is very upset though, because the landlord has acquired a bull terrier, which is quite untrained and eager to play with James. He does not appreciate the animal and refuses to be knocked over whenever he goes out.

I took a car down to see my old friend in hospital last Sunday; I have to have cars occasionally because of my bad eyesight. I found him rather sad as the doctors are going to amputate his leg. He is a good fellow and one feels very sorry for him. I do hope you are keeping well and do not find the extra work tiring. If Beatrice has written any more articles, Clare and I would like to see one; we did like that in which she gave some extracts about this country. Clare sends her love, as do I, and very best wishes for the New Year, with no horrid war to come. With much love, Emilie.

1951

Lavender Cottage.   March 4th 1951

Dear Marion and Beatrice,

It seems a long time since I wrote; you would have heard from us earlier if that wretched flu had not laid hold on us. We took it in turns, luckily, so we were able to nurse each other. We do hope you have both escaped it and also Cousin Ethel, it is an unpleasant thing and this year it specialises in a new and prolonged sort. However, all's well, etc. We are all enjoying your nice things and a great boon they are just now, when the government seems to be having a game with provisions. I have just visited a poor old soul who is trying to keep up a good fire without trespassing too much on her hundredweight of coal. It is so very hard on the poor people but I must say they keep smiling.

Do you remember my mentioning the Countess Brassey who used to preside at our invalid home meetings? She passed away last week, just before our annual meeting; she was a grand old lady although one couldn't hear a word she said. Clare and I were very thrilled a few evening ago when a Mr LW Brockington gave a paper on The Festival of Britain, it was called, "A Canadian Looks at the Festival of Britain."; it was most interesting. We made a silly remark afterwards. I said: "Do you think Marion and Beatrice know him?" Clare said: "I wonder." Then we laughed, remembering the size of Canada!

I must tell you about my birthday, which occurred a little time ago. Edith Lake's sister made a birthday cake with 80 tiny candles on it; all lighted up, and invited us to a very nice lunch. I was just over the flu and Clare was just starting it when we went. In spite of that we enjoyed the lunch and still more the cake. The same week the little church sent us two lovely pots of flowers and members sent numbers of cards. It seemed quite worthwhile to be 80! I am sorry to say that James is not over well. His abscess is larger and he finds difficulty in swallowing. However, I must say he does justice to his food. I haven't found a suitable journal to send you yet but am still on the look out. Much love to you both and may the east wind give you a merciful miss!
Yours affectionately, Emilie

1951

Dear Angelique,

January 1951 brought spells of snow and rain, punctuated by one of those freaky winter days we still get, when spring puts in a brief appearance. This yielded a jolly, Hastings newspaper picture of laughing boys paddling in the sea. It's not surprising Emilie mentions the further cut in meat ration; it was down to 4 ounces, the lowest it had ever been. This is 4 ounces per week, not per day! Thirteen people's ration books would have been required to buy a leg of lamb. Cooper-Key, Hastings' Member of Parliament criticised the government on this subject saying that the people who are poorly off for food are those who cannot afford to get a restaurant meal off the ration, when their allocated food was finished in a day or two.

Emilie's "I hope there is no horrid war to come", reference does not give the real impression of how the conflict in Korea was dominating the news. The BBC was so concerned at the prospect of a war that they put their newsreaders on a wartime footing; reducing their number to 8 and to those whose voices would be easily recognised. Newsreaders with dialects or women were not allowed; it was considered that these did not have enough gravitas to deliver news of momentous events. Perhaps you can see, Angelique, from whence some of my generation got their stuffy attitudes and how revolutionary the sixties were for us.

February brought heavy rain and flooding to Hastings, the whole country experienced the wettest February since 1870; coal and coke prices went up as a winter fuel shortage grew more acute. Hastings Corporation announced that it was prepared to grant mortgages under the Small Dwellings Acquisition Act, to help people to buy homes. The maximum value of the house should not exceed £5,000 and the rate of interest was 3.25%. The Hollington area of the town had 116 newly-built council houses but there were still 1755 families on the local housing register.

Well, the poor old countess did not whisper her way through the 1951 convalescent home AGM; she died on the day Emilie was celebrating her 80th birthday, Wednesday 21st February. The news of her death was considered to be of considerable importance locally and it took up a large part of the front page of the following Saturday's Hastings and

St Leonards Observer. The article included a picture of Lady Idina, Viscountess Hythe and Countess Brassey; a tiny lady, dressed in a mannish get up, which made her look like an elderly gentleman. The attributes and achievements of this lady, who was remarkable for her times, were impressive. Her girlhood love of cricket and fox hunting had earned her the family nickname, 'Jack'. She had travelled widely throughout the British Empire with her late husband, Thomas Allnut Brassey. During the First World War, in connection with her work with the Red Cross, she turned the family home, Normanhurst, near Battle, into a military hospital and became its commandant. She was a personal friend of Queen Mary and it is believed that she and King George V visited Lady Idina's home, Park Gate, in 1930, when the royal couple stayed at Eastbourne.

Lady Idina's life was devoted to the community; she was a Justice of the Peace and a Parish Councillor and an active patron of many charities and institutions, hence her support of St Catherine's Convalescent Home, where Emilie encountered her. It seems Emilie did not attend any obsequies; St Catherine's was represented by the committee chairwoman, Miss B Muller, at a St Leonards' requiem mass. I learned from a woman who had been a 14 year-old servant to Lady Idina, that the whispery voice Emilie mentioned was not an affliction of age, the countess had always spoken softly and was very good to servants. She was known for her intense, kindly interest in everyone and unfailing sense of humour. So you see, she was certainly like Emilie in this way; I think they would have got on well, given the chance.

My own life at that time was very curious; weekdays I was a scruffy, badly dressed, pigtailed, grammar school girl and at the weekends, grown up and dressed up, ready to go out on outings, motorbike rides, the cinema and shows at the White Rock Pavilion. In January I saw there the world famous Indian dancer, Ram Gopal at the White Rock; his exotic appearance and dress and the erotic music and movements were a bit of a shock to a Hastings audience!
Love from Victoria

1951

Lavender Cottage.   March 18th 1951

Dear Marion and Beatrice

Thank you for your letter. We are so sorry you have again been a victim of the flu. It seems a special kind this time; both Clare and I felt very owlish after our turns. We hope you have really recovered before going out. We have sustained the longest bout of rain ever known and as the garden is soaked it seems useless to begin planting anything yet. It is good of you to think of food for us. You should have seen Clare's face when the butcher brought our meat portion; three bones with a reddish mist over them. But she has turned it into broth, which will be very nourishing she says. We have some of your lovely chicken left and so are independent of the butcher's contribution.

It is humorous to see the Minister of Food's provision list and the way he puts up prices is terrific. I hope that inflation won't follow. Still, we have four crocuses out and there is the promise of some daffodils. If our landlord doesn't run his garage through it, the front garden will not be too bad.

I am very glad that you like the Everybody's as Clare thinks it is quite good and it is so difficult to get good journals at present. We have tried several but they are mainly about fashion or cookery and I am sure you know all about those. I hope Beatrice is having a very successful journey for her paper. She writes so well and makes her articles interesting. We send our love to you both, with all best wishes for your speedy recovery. Mind you are careful. If your weather is like ours, it is enough to make you want to build an ark. James would send love, if he wasn't asleep but his years are telling on him (16) and his interests lie in food and slumber.
Yours, Emilie

1951

Lavender Cottage.   April 18th 1951.

Dear Marion and Beatrice,

The parcels arrived today. Hurrah! What a lot of lovely things, we feel quite overcome at your kindness. We certainly shall not starve for a long time; there are one or two others who would thank you if they could. I have just taken some slices of bacon over to a very old lady and she is so pleased. The bacon here is indifferent and tough. I know you don't want too many thanks but the things really are a Godsend.

There is no fresh news to give you. I think that everyone regrets the loss of Bevan, even if they did not agree with his politics; he and Sir Stafford Cripps were good men and there seem to be so few of their kind left. The talk here is of a General Election; there is so much dissatisfaction but I doubt whether there will be much change. The work people will be very upset by the regulations regarding betting and pools, which are rampant. I am glad they are trying to sober these; so many people spend money on them in the hopes of enormous prizes.

I am sorry to say I had to give up the secretary-ship of the convalescent home on account of deafness and bad eyesight. I cannot hear well enough to take the minutes but I hope to be able to do something helpful still. The members are so kind to me and it really is a good home. It was not taken over by the state as so many of its kind.

I am so glad you liked Everybody's, so many of the old journals have been discontinued owing, I suppose, to the shortage of paper. This is a short letter as I want to let you know about the parcels. I am giving this to the postman to save time, he is a kindly soul.
With much love, Emilie.

1951

Dear Angelique,

The loss of Bevan Emilie mentions was not his death, but his resignation from the cabinet, over the planned charges for National Health teeth and glasses. He retired to the Commons back benches, where he was joined by two other ministers, one of whom was Harold Wilson, a future Prime Minister. This was a major blow to the stability of the Labour government, which had a very small majority. They had previously been defeated on March 2nd by four votes, after a Commons debate on the shortage of raw materials. You can see why Emilie mentioned the possibility of a General Election.

After the brief reference to the talk on the Festival of Britain, Emilie does not mention it again but it was a tremendous event for the country. The King inaugurated the festival on May 4th, 1951, one hundred years after the Victorian Great Exhibition. Austerity was far from over but the Festival of Britain Exhibition, built on 27 acres of bomb-damaged London, was a symbol of faith in the future. The Festival of Britain was also a showcase for emerging trends in architectural and other forms of engineering and the use of new materials in building and it introduced fresh, exciting designs in furniture, textiles and ceramics. I know you love collecting little things, Angelique; it might be worth while to look out for 1950's items of tableware and bric-a-brac. I like them for their clean, elliptical shapes and 'space age' patterns in primary colours.

Hastings Corporation felt that it should respond to the spirit of Festival of Britain Year and they agreed that buildings on the seafront should be painted up. Concern was expressed about the still existing bomb damage sites and the solution for these eyesores was to hide them from public scrutiny behind hastily erected, painted walls. Further money was spent on more plants and bulbs for the seafront flower beds and decorative illuminations; the latter proved to be a disappointment because they were easily outshone by the street lighting.

The highlight of the year was the May 19th visit to Hastings by Princess Elizabeth and the town turned out on a day of sunshine and cloud to give her a rousing welcome. The Princess crammed a big

116

programme of duties into the day, which included laying a foundation stone, visiting the town hall, being presented with a silver winkle pin by the Winkle Club and receiving the deeds of Hastings Castle and those of the Fairlight and Ecclesbourne Glens. I know you have met veteran web site builder Ivor White, well, he was a Hastings-based freelance press photographer at that time. He said Her Royal Highness kept him on his toes all day as he took pictures, developed them, rushed them to the train for London and then hurried back to photograph her at the next assignment. As I write to you, we are 11 days away from celebrating Queen Elizabeth's Golden Jubilee and Her Majesty is involved in a tour of the entire country, carrying out the same kind duties that she has done for over fifty years. Another trooper, like Emilie!
Love from Victoria

Lavender Cottage.   July 24th 1951

Dear Marion and Beatrice,

So many thanks for your kind letter, which I should have answered days ago but my time was taken up with looking after Clare, escorting her to hospital for x-rays and to see a special man who understands mouth complaints. It appears to be an abscess, which has made its way up the throat and is painful in the extreme. However, the doctors, we have a visiting one as well, give great hope of an early recovery. She has daily injections and this week, on Wednesday, we go again for what I hope is the final opinion. Clare manages to eat fairly well with the nice things you have sent, putting her teeth in for meals only, by orders. I shall hope to give you more satisfactory news in my next.

It was very interesting to have your news of Emily, I remember her so well; she was very kindly and practical. I never forget her remarks when she was returning home, I think, taking France by air on the way. Clar'Em'ly said to her: 'You must be careful', she retorted: 'It's for them to be careful, not me!' I also remember Mr Frank; he was such a gentle, kindly man. It was interesting too, to read about Miss Mayford and the old brick house. It makes one glad to read of her briskness when over 80; it shows that age is not a bar to energy. Two of our friends from London have just spent a fortnight in Hastings. One is just over 90 and lamed by an accident but her head is perfectly clear. She is treasurer of one of our churches, keeping accounts and writing as legibly as ever. Some of these old folks put youngsters to shame, as you say.

Thank you so much for suggestions of flour and sugar. The former is quite cook-able still, the latter, limited periodically but not too sparse. A little soap would be an advantage as what comes is a little tough and has no flavour, if one may apply those words to soap! We are still enjoying that nice money gift. It is difficult to find things for Clare as she always says that she doesn't want anything, but I have discovered that more stockings would be advantageous, so I am getting those for her, hoping she will let out another want shortly.

Now that I cannot do the secretary's work at the convalescent home I am repairing their books, which are in a bad state. The resident folk do an amount of reading when the weather is poor. I hope to hear of your successful journey to Cape Cod. I must look it up on the map you sent, for it sounds as if it were a very long way. The parcels sound most attractive; you are both so very, very kind. We both send much love and good wishes.
Yours affectionately, Emilie.

Lavender Cottage.   August 6th 1951.

Dear Marion and Beatrice,

Clar' Em'ly keeps on saying that I have not acknowledged the lovely parcels that came on the 2nd. I said that I had done so but she is persistent and no doubt her memory is better than mine. Anyway, it is a pleasure to write to you though I can't always trust the offers of posting I receive. We have already plunged into meat and butter but there is such a lovely lot; we shall be sustained for a long time.

We don't want to grumble but there seems to be a great deal of 'syntheticism' (if that is the right word) here and your gifts are so nice that we get real enjoyment from meals. They are more welcome than ever as Clare's mouth is still so bad and it is good to see her enjoying her food. We see the specialist again tomorrow and I do hope he will do something to alleviate the pain.

I do hope that you don't mind, but I am donating a little of your last monetary gift to a subscription to the Animals Day this month. I am sure you will agree with me; I can't bear to hear of the poor things being neglected and sometimes cruelly treated, not always by natural cruelty but ignorance. You see, James is always considered and humoured; one feels so much for the strays, one comes here to be fed every day.

I do hope you will have the holiday you mentioned and that good weather will prevail.
Please excuse bad writing; I hope to have new glasses this month, the eyes being rather trying. Why don't they make air letters from white paper?
Much love from Emilie.

Dear Angelique,

It's very evident that Clare was becoming very unwell but Emilie continued optimistic, or is she hiding her anxiety?

With reference to food; the flour situation had improved in this country but in the spring the Ministry of Food had announced higher prices for flour. Bakers were able to produce a greater range of cakes but had to increase prices, including for the bread round delivery charge, which went up to 3d (1p) per family. Soap supplies were still a bit of a problem; in my family we used only household soap in the bathroom; I think the main reason for this was because scented soap was seen by my father as being rather effeminate, his only concession to a 'scent' was carbolic! I did have a small bar of wallflower perfumed soap, which I used before romantic outings with John, for romantic was what they had become.

All the spring and summer of 1951 I had been having confrontations with my parents about school. I had disliked the school system since I was small. Because of the outbreak of war in 1939 and the resulting social upheaval, my first experience of schooling had been in the kitchen of an elderly and retired headmistress, in company with four other "starters". She was strict but kindly; we used to giggle at the sight of her vast drawers, drying over the kitchen range. Real school never matched up to this homely beginning; my speech and manner made me an oddity in the class and I was sometimes bullied. When I grew older I was a frequent truant; while my mother was at work I stayed at home, reading and writing.

At sixteen I was fed up with being a school child, when I thought I was almost grown up. I had nurtured ambitions to be a writer but these ideas were abandoned in the quest for "real" adulthood. The grammar school headmistress was scathing in her comments to me when I left school in early July 1951, saying, with eyes half closed in scorn, "We do not educate you here to be well-spoken shop girls", for that is what I was to be, at the Hastings department store, Plummer Roddis. As I walked out of the school gates for the last time I threw my hated brown felt hat in a ditch. John and I attended the wedding of my brother Ron to Phyllis on July 28th and, no longer a school-girl, I drank wine and felt grown up at last!

In the 50s, the August Bank Holiday Weekend was at the beginning of August, not at the end, as now. Hastings was still enjoying its post-war revival as a holiday destination; the cheap, continental package holidays that were to ruin the town as a resort were some years distant. The promenade was filled with seaside attractions for all ages; miniature trains, trams and coaches, a children's play land, an open air swimming pool and the indoor White Rock Baths, twice daily concerts on the pier bandstand and music and tea dancing in the Sun Lounge and White Rock Pavilion. The black and white minstrels performed on the beach; nobody had heard of political correctness then. For the sporting there were a gymkhana, water polo and an aqua show. And, of course, all the traditional, glorious, day trippers' pleasures of fish and chips, winkles and whelks, peppermint rock, postcards, sea-paddling and funny hats. People really did love to be beside the seaside at Hastings.

August also saw the demolition of Normanhurst, the one-time home of the late Countess Brassey. It was a lovely building; it had the look of a fairy-tale castle. I have a print of a water colour of it painted by a German prisoner, who was held at the detention camp there in WWII. Love from Victoria

Lavender Cottage.   September 10th 1951.

Dear Marion and Beatrice,

Please excuse me not writing earlier but I am waiting to hear some definite news of Clare. It seems such a long time before the doctors decide and the hospital at Westminster is three hours away. I was there last Wednesday and I am going tomorrow. Clare is very cheerful; I do hope things will turn out well but it is a nasty wound in her mouth and very painful. I will let you know as soon as I hear. Do excuse this brief note.
Much love to you both, Emilie

Lavender Cottage.   September 20th 1951

Dear Marion and Beatrice,

I really don't know how to thank you for the lovely present, it was beyond everything and I must tell you to what it is being devoted. I had to go to the hospital four times by train or an ambulance, which they sent twice. I found the train journey so tiring, we had to get to the station first, quite some distance. I said to Clare last week that I really must go another way as this is very tiring as it takes three hours each way. She suggested a car, so much dearer, of course, but we decided to have one, though we felt rather bad over it. Then, came your letter and enclosure, so I went by car. I felt so luxurious and you can imagine it was most comfortable; from door to door, both ways. C thinks it is just lovely of you and of course I do too.

Clare's mouth is a little better and the doctor thinks a few weeks will finish it. They don't tell us what it is but just say that it is some kind of growth in the mouth, climbing up to the head. She is very well looked after and the Westminster Hospital is a lovely place. She is in the pyrotherapy ward and there are some very nice patients there. I take your letters to her to read and she sends lots of love and messages to you. She says she can eat the meat you sent as it is so tender.

You would laugh at my cooking. You see Clare has done it hitherto and I feel quite strange at it but I am getting on. We still have some of the butter and meat you sent; I am keeping them till she returns. I had a large haddock today but it wasn't like the haddocks we got years back. I expect my taste has changed but even James refused it. He, poor boy, has had to have the vet, a nice man, who came three times; he gave James up at first but on the third occasion he thought James would get another year as he had begun to eat. His appetite now is awful, one can hardly give him enough.

I am glad to hear you had such a good holiday and that you so thoroughly enjoyed it. CE said, 'So they ought to have a lovely time, they always want others to have one'.Please forgive writing. I had to get new glasses for both reading and sight and I am not quite used to them yet.

Lots of love and again, many, many thanks to you. Emilie

Dear Angelique,

Poor Emilie and Clare, their life at Lavender Cottage is unravelling so horribly and it is wretched for them both that Clare has had to go to a London hospital. I have researched the subject of the Westminster Hospital and eventually found an American web site that had a potted history of a Westminster Hospital founded in 1834. There is a picture of a grand and gloomy-looking building, which was demolished in 1950 to make way for the Queen Elizabeth II Conference Centre. But here, in Emilie's letters it is 1951 and Clare is in the Westminster Hospital, perhaps the web site writer got the date wrong.

1951

Once again the Canadian cousin comes to the rescue with a practical gift of money. I investigated the cost of rail and hire car travel for this period; a rail ticket from Hastings to Charing Cross, third class return, was 13/3 and a chauffer driven car to London £3/17/6 return, (66p and £3.85). To put this in perspective, a working man's wage was about £4.10.00 (£4.50) per week at that time. I am informed that the train journey to London was better in 1951 than it is today; the trains were more safe and punctual and as for road travel, it was most enjoyable, no M25 traffic jams. No wonder Emilie felt luxurious going by car. She must have felt very lonely and weary.
Love from Victoria.

Lavender Cottage.   September 27th 1951.

Dear Marion and Beatrice,

Thank you so much for your most kind letter. I wanted to see Clare again before answering. I went on Wednesday to see her and found her not so well, which was disappointing. I have not heard from her today and I am trying to find the regulations for telephoning the Westminster Hospital. Clare thought your letter was the kindest in the world. I have no information about the throat, which she said was again paining her. She wants to get home and enjoy some of the nice things you have sent. The patients take in nothing but nightdresses and wraps for moving about, otherwise all is provided. It's a lovely hospital; I should say the most efficient in England. You may have noticed that His Majesty the King has nurses from there, also doctors. I must say that they are most kind to her but of course she gets homesick. I do wish she were nearer; we can only go on Wednesdays and Sundays for 1½ hours between 2.00pm-3.30pm. Her niece goes once or twice as she is something in the government but I go on Wednesdays. Sundays there is a mob; others go when they can. I shall certainly let you know of her improvements. I can't help feeling anxious; she writes or sends a card every day. I am expecting the arrival of a visitor who will find out about telephoning for me.

Clare has asked if you can spare a couple of pillowslips as she would be very glad of them when she comes home. I don't know when that will be but I don't think they will let her go before complete recovery. We can't do anything about food at present, all patients have the same; it is quite good, even if it is not that which she prefers. She said she longed to get home and be eating some of your nice tins of beef with real gravy!

Later, on the 29th

Glad to say I have had five letters; they were delayed. Clare was quite cheerful but I am afraid it is a long job. I will let you know all news; I am trying to catch the post with this.

Yours affectionately, Emilie.

Lavender Cottage.   October 25th 1951

Dear Marion and Beatrice,

Your lovely box of soap arrived this morning and I was so sorry that Clar'Em'ly was not here to see it. It will last a very long time and will be thoroughly enjoyed by us. I will tell Clare about it when I go to the hospital, which will probably be Sunday, though trains are very bad that day. I fear I cannot give you very good news of her, although the cheeks have been cured the illness has gone to the throat. It is uncertain when they will let her come home, though they talk of two weeks. She is quite cheerful but having no teeth it is awkward to eat so she has been living on bananas and beaten up egg; she has lost so much weight and one cannot help but feel anxious.

I have had the part of the house that is ours done up to look nice and keep hoping all will be well. They talk of sending her home by stretcher as she could not sit up in a car. To be quite honest, my dear cousins, I do feel quite anxious; they won't tell us what it is, which makes it worse. But I must not depress you, but 60 years of friendship is a long time, isn't it? It is unfortunate her hospital is so far from here. I would have gone and lived near but Clare was against it as she can only be visited for a very little time on Wednesdays and Sundays. She is having the best attention in every way; the king's doctors and nurses. This is a dismal letter but I hope for better next time.

Much love to you both, Emilie

1951

Dear Angelique,

Although we accepted it then, knowing nothing different, being in hospital in the 1950s was a little like being in prison; there was still a strong influence from Victorian times, regulations reigned and hospital visitors were restricted to strictly designated periods and they were sometimes seen as a nuisance; many children's hospitals actively discouraged visitors, even the child's parents.

Emilie has made no mention of current affairs in her letters; she is more concerned about Clare, James and the domestic scene. To keep you in the picture, there was a General Election on October 25th, the Conservatives were returned to power and Churchill to Number 10, promising to make Britain, "strong and free". A twenty-six year old Conservative candidate, the youngest in the country, a certain Miss Margaret Roberts, did not win in her constituency; a sleeping tigress, as time would reveal!
Love from Victoria

Lavender Cottage.   November 9th 1951

 Dear Marion and Beatrice,

I am so glad to tell you Clar' Em'ly has taken a turn for the better and was able to come home yesterday. Of course, she is very poorly and keeps in bed. The mouth is still sore and she will have to go to Westminster for inspection in a month. She does look a poor little thing in bed, with painted cheeks and so thin. She can eat only milky things because she has no teeth and she will not get them for some time. But it is nice to have her back and if only the mouth will keep better she will be all right. They said it was a malignant growth and she has had no end of electricity or whatever poured into her. Do excuse my handwriting but I want the postman to take this. Clare sends her love to you both as do I.
Love from Emilie

1951

Dear Angelique,

Emilie must have been overjoyed to have Clare at home but one fears Clare has been discharged from the hospital, not because she has taken a turn for the better but because no more can really be done for her. The prognosis is discouraging but of course this would not be acknowledged in those days and certainly Emilie would always hope for the best. No news of the world outside Lavender Cottage with this one, it does not seem appropriate somehow.
Love from Victoria'

Lavender Cottage.   November 13th 1951

Dear Marion and Beatrice,

Your lovely parcels arrived safely; I know how much we shall enjoy them. Clare is revelling in the soup as her mouth at present debars anything else. She is delighted with the pillow cases but says you should not have sent her two. She has been home since Thursday and is very glad to be here again, though no one could be kinder than the hospital people. I have to take her in a month for inspection; I am not sorry to have a little respite; the journey to the hospital takes two and a half hours each way and one gets only one and a half hours with her.

Neighbours are very good and keep calling to ask how she is but one must not allow much talking, of course. Two neighbours lent us beds so that she would not have to go upstairs and we keep big fires going. I don't believe I answered much of your last letter, did I acknowledge the soap? It is wicked for me to ask for anything else but in some time, a long time, will you pop in a tiny bit of cheese for me? What we get is tasteless and hard. Please forgive my asking for it. I might have mentioned that CE cannot take anything salty at present but that will go off later.
Yours affectionately, Emilie.

1951

Lavender Cottage.   December 7th 1951.

Dear Marion and Beatrice,

Your exciting telegram arrived just as we were starting off for the hospital, where Clar'Emily was to be inspected. I signed it quickly and took it with me, to forward it from Westminster but the post office there did not take telegrams from abroad. So I brought it back to our Hastings office. You should have heard the post office man here laugh. "You've signed it the wrong way round; we'll soon put that right". He was a nice man. He said: "Is that all you want to say? You can get twenty words for what they have paid!" My experience of our telegrams is an allocation of about ten words, including the address. So I made a few suggestions, which he supplemented, though we did not quite meet his longing to use every syllable allowed. I felt he would not be unwilling to put in a word or two on his own account! Anyway, I hope the wire arrived safely after all these vicissitudes. His parting words were: "I shall look out for a slice of that turkey!" He was a nice old man.

I am glad to say that the doctors' (three of them) report, was very favourable and Clare will not report again for three months. She has a good deal of pain still but they seem to have destroyed the worst part. I said: 'Will you be able to eat the turkey?' She replied that she would if it was cut up very small but we could make broth of the bones. She became quite excited over it and said that we could give old Mrs Smith some turkey, also the parrot lady, etc. So I argue that the bird will be of great interest to many. It is a pity James' taste is so low; he prefers cod.

We have just been very extravagant. It is very trying to light fires of late, owing to the very inferior coal we have now, so we decided to imitate some of our neighbours and buy a stove that never goes out; I expect you have had these for a long time. It didn't cost much and so far it has been going for two days, needing only a moderate amount of coal and the removal of the ashes, which are held in a tray and can be taken away easily. It will certainly save coal, if nothing else and keeps the room warm day and night.

1951

I have not thanked you yet for the papers you sent. We thought the pictures were very good and we are glad that the Princess had such a good welcome. Did I tell you our next door neighbour, Miss Feather, has gone to live in Yorkshire? We miss her very much, she was always very kind. Her house has been taken by a retired canon and his wife. I tell James he must be a respectable cat and not trespass on their territory. I am to make a formal call next week; I think they are quite homely folks.

Do forgive writing; I am writing in bed. I could not do any yesterday as CE's nephew came to see her today and took up time. He is quite a nice man and insisted on paying some of her hospital expenses. Of course she objected and said she would pay her own but she had to give in at last. We both send you much love and every good wish for Christmas.

Much love from Emilie

Dear Angelique,

Isn't it good to see Emilie's sense of humour re-emerging? I loved the account of her interchange with the post office clerk; I bet he did get some turkey too! It seems Clare was a private, paying patient in Westminster Hospital but if she had a civil service pension maybe that was not beyond her reach. So, they have a retired canon as a new neighbour. I have learned he was Rev. Canon James Morgan, M.A. D.D. Perhaps the house was church property, for the use of retired clergy.

The newspapers sent to Lavender Cottage from Canada had obviously reported the visit of Princess Elizabeth and Prince Phillip in October; the King was not well enough to make this visit as scheduled. He had been ailing for some months and was diagnosed in early September as suffering from lung disease, for which he underwent surgery on September 23rd. Emilie's remark about the King's doctors now falls into place. Princess Elizabeth was given a rapturous welcome in Canada; she and her sister Princess Margaret were just as adored in their time as Princess Diana.

1951

In November, John took me to the Rye Town Guy Fawkes' celebrations, which was considered second only to the Battle bonfire in those days. There was a procession of floats, people in fancy dress, flaming torches, fireworks and a huge bonfire on Rye Salts. This is all pretty standard stuff these days but like many who grew up during the war I had seen nothing like it and felt as thrilled as a little child; I still do, on these occasions. An unusual feature of Rye's bonfire event was the cooking and selling of smoked pilchards in the street; we ate them with our fingers, in half darkness, swallowing fins, scales, bones and all. I have a very precious snapshot of that night, taken by a roving street photographer.
With love from Victoria.

Lavender Cottage.   December 22nd 1951.

 Dear Marion and Beatrice,

This is just to acknowledge the safe arrival of the turkey amid much rejoicing. He is a lovely bird and Clar'Em'ly is thinking of the delicious gravy she will be able to enjoy as well as the tender meat. A neighbour, an expert in dealing with large poultry, is coming in a little while to dissect him as he outreaches our stove limits a little but that will not matter. There are also a few other folks who will rejoice in him, the poorer folk cannot aspire to poultry. We were anxious after your last letter in case the turkey did not turn up and our thanks will fly to you with every mouthful. Do excuse my scrawl but I want to post this as soon as possible; the posts in this place are very bad. We both send our love and many, many thanks. I hope you will think of us on Tuesday.
Love from Emilie

Lavender Cottage.   December 26th 1951.

Dear Marion and Beatrice,

Two such lovely parcels have arrived and have been opened with great excitement; you are too good! We shall certainly not be hungry for ages and I am so glad to say that Clare could eat a bit of minced turkey. We gave a substantial amount to the old lady opposite and I will distribute some more as soon as I can get out; the rain is very bad. We did so enjoy unpacking the parcels; you do pack beautifully. I feel that we now have provisions for months, for ourselves and to share with others. The parrot's mistress was overjoyed with the bird seed for Laura; that which we get here is very poor so the packet was a god send. I am always delighted with handkerchiefs, colds are prevalent these days. I am enjoying the tea you sent, it is much nicer than that which you can buy here. Your generosity allows us to give some to those who are heavy tea drinkers but have limited rations. We are allowed extra tea because of our age. It is a pity Clare cannot drink any tea but china but as her idea of tea is a very small half-teaspoon it doesn't make much difference

Our old lady, who has been coming to "clean up" for us, had a kind of fit and can come no more. I expect we will have Mrs Todd, the parrot's owner instead. She is rather a doleful person but a good worker. We received about 70 Christmas cards and many letters of sympathy for Clare, which she did not feel equal to answering, so I have written close on 90 replies. All the folks round here are very nice and many eggs have been sent to Clare. She sends you her love and says I am to tell you how much she enjoyed her piece of turkey. We will make broth of the leftovers. I join with her in love and thanks and hope that the New Year will be a very, very happy one for you.
Emilie

Dear Angelique,

There was so much upheaval this year in Lavender Cottage and now, the going of the cleaning lady of 14 years service, otherwise known as

the Blitz. Can you imagine the bustle in the kitchen and among the neighbours of Lavender Cottage in the preparation of the splendid turkey? Emilie's immediate concerns about accommodation had subsided and just as well too. The housing shortage remained serious in Hastings and had been the subject of local news throughout the year. Rock Lane, Winchelsea Road, Pine Avenue and Hollington were proposed as sites of new council house schemes costing £60,000. The council were also considering requisitioning private housing, if the owners did not rent or sell them.

The war in Korea continued, many austerity conditions remained in effect in Britain, most basic foods were still rationed or in short supply. As an unwelcome Christmas present to Hastings householders, domestic coal was increased by 8/1d (40p) per ton. My mother, helped by government farm workers' food supplements, made a wonderful spread for Christmas Day. All the men in my family over-indulged in beer and sherry on Christmas Eve and were slightly subdued company on the 25th. I did not mind, John was not much of a drinker and it was a happy day for us both. I had a surprise parcel in the post that Christmas; it was my battered, old school hat, complete with its silvery, metal badge, rescued from the ditch and sent as a little prank, from my former school friends. I did not know that my mother kept that badge for decades until she gave it to me, a few years before she died aged 98. I understand now how disappointed she must have been by my failure to continue my education and realize my ambition. The child in me wants to say, 'Hey, look Mum, I'm writing a book'!
Love from Victoria

1952

Lavender Cottage.   January 3rd 1952.

My Dear Friends and Cousins,

There! I ought to have said "our" as Clar'Em'ly thinks of herself in that capacity. We have too much to thank you for; the Christmas parcels arrived safely, I thank you for that, and today a luxurious cheese has made its appearance. All this reminds me of a Grimm's fairy tale; wish and a gift appears. It's no use my thanking you for individual (is that the right word?) gifts, for there are so many and all so acceptable. Do you know I enjoy the white and coloured handkerchiefs immensely? The coloured ones are especially attractive and save my laundry no end. Which reminds me, (excuse this pen, it is so vile), our poor old char has had to leave us after twenty years. She fell down our staircase last week and she can do no more work. We are sorry; she was a good worker though her efforts, so to speak, were limited. Her successor is the parrot's mistress, who does not share the bird's profanity. She was very moved and rejoiced at the seed. So did the parrot though her language was more suggestive of a pirate craft than of any respectable establishment!

I am sorry to say that CE is not much better, but she was able to enjoy a nice lot of turkey broth. Her throat is still painful and I am afraid it will mean another stay at the Westminster Hospital. She is to see another doctor here this week but he can only advise as the hospitals here have no facilities for the treatment she requires. It is very disheartening and she feels it, though remaining cheerful.

James is very well and enjoys his fish with great ardour. He sleeps downstairs near my bed and wakes me punctually at 6.00am with a demand to go out. We had to get small beds for the rooms here as ours were very large and I believe James thinks that it is all done for his benefit. Clar' Em'ly sends much love to you both and says heaven has been kind to her in allowing her to know you. She is sound asleep now and I shall put her to bed soon as she gets so tired.
Much love to you both and we wish you the Happy New Year you deserve. Emilie.

1952

Lavender Cottage.   January 27th 1952.

My Dear Cousins,

I have been trying to write for some days but we seem to have hordes of people visiting, very nice of them but it does hinder correspondence. To make matter worse, I broke my sight glasses last week and find they have to go north for repairs so I can't see very well to write. You so kindly asked whether Clare wanted anything specially. She says I ought not to tell you but she would be very glad of some dried milk. The milk suppliers limit us in that respect and as her food is all milky we do use a lot. I do feel very bad in mentioning it as you are good to us beyond all description. I think Clare is a little better but of course the throat is not over good and the nurse comes every day to paint it. I am glad to say that Clare can eat a little porridge if I boil it all night; she enjoys broth made from meaty things too, which varies her diet. I think she is better, although outsiders are very gloomy about her illness. She saw the doctor here again but he said he could do nothing. That did not worry me as he has not the apparatus that they have at Westminster. Did I tell you that we have embarked on a new stove to keep in all night? I think I did. I have come to the conclusion that it isn't much of a gain as the other stove keeps in by heaping it with slack over night and doesn't burn half the coal.

James has been somewhat of a trial this week and the vet we called in thought he ought to be put to sleep, he is 17, but we could not bear it and hope he will get another lease of life. Of course, it is awkward to be aroused at 3.00 a.m. to let him out but he is a good cat and sings very gratefully for any kindness. Would Beatrice be good enough to let me have something about Labrador? I have been trying to describe the occasion when we were nearly wrecked by an iceberg but I can't remember whether Labrador was an asset in that case. I remember being tossed on the floor and a wailing passenger moaning at my side. I know it's a strange thing to ask but I want to write a description if I can. Excuse my writing, I can't see well with my old glasses.
Yours affectionately, Emilie.

1952

Dear Angelique,

You will gather that Britain was still suffering food rationing in 1952, in fact new austerity measures were introduced by the government in January, which included more National Health Service charges. We see another change in the Lavender Cottage household with the departure of the Blitz. It's odd that just now Emilie refers to a terrifying incident in her travels. If only she had given a date, Labrador would be an asset in my case! It has been suggested to me I could fictionalize Emilie's story but I would not want to change or add to a thing about her, would you?
  Love from Victoria

Lavender Cottage.   February 18th 1952,

 Our Dear Cousins,

We are feeling just a little better now that things are quieter and the Queen elected satisfactorily. To tell the truth, we did feel apprehensive about her journey home. It would have been sad if anything had happened to her, would it not, as the little boy is so young?

Clare says that I am not thanking you enough for the lovely things you have sent. Without the least exaggeration I can say that they have kept us alive for we could never have managed to buy the things in England now that the pound is worth so little. The coffee you sent is delicious, the dried milk invaluable, we still have plenty. Clare says that from her point of view the best is the Hedgeland beef; the gravy is delicious, no salt or anything, so she has this and I have the meat; a most fair division that suits us both. But it's all lovely! I could go on for ever telling you about the things; didn't the parrot enjoy her share! Her mistress is now doing some work for us as it was getting so wearing, bringing in coals for two fires.

Clare does not improve much, though the doctor keeps saying the mouth is better. I shall be glad when she goes for inspection at Westminster as the doctors here have no facilities for a proper examination. What dreadful writing this is and I do dislike this bluish paper; I'm sure no one can read it. James has had the vet again; I fear he is getting beyond things. We shall be sorry as he is a good cat. I must rise up now and get C the hot water bottle as she is so cold day and night. However she is cheerful and sleeps very well. She can drink but not eat. She sends much love to you both in which I join, of course, so would James if he knew.

Much love to you both, Emilie,

Dear Angelique,

I think it is a sign of Emilie's anxiety and occupation with Clare that she makes only a passing reference to the death of King George VI, which occurred on 6th February. Princess Elizabeth was in Kenya when he died, fulfilling duties her father had been too ill to carry out; hence her remark about the journey home. To a person of Emilie's age, the rituals surrounding and national response to a royal death were not new experiences but for me they were overwhelming. My mother told me that the news of King George's death was not as dramatically received as that of Queen Victoria's. My mother was six years old when this happened and she said that she recalled that even members of the public wore black. My mother lived in London then and her much older brother took her to see Queen Victoria's funeral cortege pass through the streets; she particularly remembered the great black carriage horses, their heads decorated with black ostrich plumes.

When King George VI died, the department store, Plummer Roddis, where I was working as a shop assistant, dressed its display windows in black, as did all other shops. BBC radio broadcast only solemn music between news bulletins. The Hastings and St Leonards Observer's front page had black-edged columns and was full of pictures of local dignitaries observing civic and mourning ceremonies. The paper carried photographs of the King as a young, uniformed, Captain HRH Prince Albert, when he visited Hastings Cricket Ground for the RAF Cadet Sports Day in 1918.

On the day of the King's funeral, saddest and most impressive to me was the picture of the three queens, standing side-by-side, Queen Mary, The Queen Mother and the new Queen Elizabeth, all dressed in deepest mourning. It looked like a scene from a Greek tragedy and made photographic history. Strange that I should find myself writing of these things to you when they are so current , with Queen Elizabeth's accession to the throne and Golden Jubilee just about to be celebrated. Love from Victoria.

Lavender Cottage.　　　　Feb 24th. 1952.

My Dear Friends,

I really don't know what to say! You are so good to us, far too good, and it's difficult to thank you sufficiently. I need not say how acceptable your gift is; it will enable us to get things that are badly wanted. For example; a suitable electric arrangement for the bedroom Clare has now. We found it was impossible to get coals enough for keeping in two fires all night. It is not that we could not pay for coals but we had reached the limit of our allowance and we had to apply for priority, which is allowed on a doctor's certificate of illness. This we had obtained but not for more coal than will last till the end of April, so we have had to cut down one fire.

Luckily, we can get wood ad lib but that does not last in a fire at night and Clar' Em'ly is so cold, in spite of hot water bottles. So we think it would be better to have an electric stove, which will be kept on all night. You can realise how nice it will be to keep the heat going. Clare keeps fairly bright though the pain does not go.

Yesterday I had an afternoon off, when a neighbour came to sit with Clare for two hours. It was the Annual General Meeting of our church and I had to go to read my year's report and, sadly, give up my secretary ship. The convalescent home position also had to be resigned. The church meeting was very nice; they said such kind things and presented me with a gorgeous pot of flowers and delightful remarks. I stayed to tea after the meeting and when I went to my car, (I must have one for my eyes) they followed me, singing," For She's a

Jolly Good Fellow". They are such nice people. We are giving a swell tea in April for the Women's Club and Literary Society, which I hope to go to if Clare is well enough. It is nice little church and they are all so kind.

I don't feel that I have thanked you adequately but I am sure you know how we feel. James does not understand why I will write letters when it is his suppertime.

Yours affectionately, Emilie,

Dear Angelique,

In spite of the severity of Clare's illness, it seems that austerity regulations were still preventing Lavender Cottage from having an adequate coal supply, so what was clearly a gift of money was put to good use.

I think I may have discovered to which church it is that Emilie refers in this letter; it is possibly St Peter's, The Ridge, Baldslow, which was about half a mile from Lavender Cottage. The church, which was considered a temporary building when it was constructed from corrugated iron in 1863, lasted for 117 years! It was an oddly attractive structure, with a tiny, wooden steeple. It gained itself the nickname the Iron Tabernacle; I have been told that when it rained during services the noise on the metal roof deafened the worshippers; it was a humble but dearly loved church. It survived until 1980, when it was demolished for a road widening scheme. The vicar of St Peters between the years 1943 to 1959 was the Rev B H Taylor and I think he may be the minister in Emilie's letters. Mentioned also in an archive newspaper article about the church was a Miss B M Cole, who was "a great worker for St Peter's". Could she be the Mrs Cole from the church, who we meet later, looking after Emilie? Perhaps either the reporter or Emilie got her marital status wrong.

The following news item gives some idea how rural The Ridge was thought to be in 1952: - A man was arrested for being in possession of

four dozen eggs, which he claimed were not stolen but had been given to him by a woman, "in the country" namely, The Ridge. Nobody would call it the country now. This also shows the extent of the continuing austerity; if a man had 48 eggs in a haversack he must be up to no good! The man was held on remand but later discharged, as no further evidence could be found. I do hope that they were not eggs from the chickens of Mrs Todd, the parrot lady.
Love from Victoria

Lavender Cottage.   March 23rd 1952.

My Dear Friends,
Unfortunately, I have no good news to tell you. Clar' Em'ly is much worse and I am afraid...

We now have two nurses as it was not possible for me to carry on and Clare needs so much attention. Her complaint is a very bad one; cancer. She came home from the hospital supposedly cured but another growth has come. She is in pain but fortunately sleeps a great deal. The nurse for the night has been very kind and the other will come this evening to take the night as the first wants to change her time to the day. I fear I am rather confused. I am writing with my ears open in case Clare calls. I would have written earlier but I have hardly a minute and I know you will forgive me. It is so sad she is going like this; I know how sorry you will be. Thanks so much for the map, safely received.
Much love to you both, Emilie

Lavender Cottage.   March 27th.1952

My Dear Cousins,

I know that you will be very sorry to hear that Clare passed away this morning.
For her I cannot grieve as she has been in so much pain for so long.
How I shall miss her I cannot imagine; 60 years is a long time, isn't it?

The nurse is so kind and is going to stay for a while. The cremation is on Monday, with a service before, at the church. You will forgive a brief note but I will write later.

Much love, Emilie.

Lavender Cottage.   April 4th 1952.

My Dear Friends and Cousins,

By this time you will have had my news but I know you will wish to have more details. Clare's death came as a great shock to me as she kept telling me of the things we should do when she was well. I found afterwards that she knew as well as the doctor did that this was the end. She was conscious right up until the end, when she went into a kind of sleep and passed away on the morning of last Thursday. Some days before she went she said: "Love to the friends in Canada".

She even prepared the notice of her own death, to be inserted in the Daily Telegraph; I could not get a copy but I remember it: - "Clare Marriott, First Class Civil Servant, died at........To be cremated at Charing....."No, I forget the rest but it was very simple and intended for the old Civil Service friends with whom she worked. I have had letters from all who remain. Her affairs were in perfect order, as you may imagine, and her nephew, who came at once, had not a difficulty in doing what was necessary. We had a nice service at the church and after, at Charing, where she was cremated, by her wish; it is about 40 miles from here. She lies close to Edith Lake, our friend who died 18 months ago. Two other old friends are in the same part. It seems hardly realisable to know that she will never sit in her armchair again and read your letters. I feel very lost and lonely, though neighbours are very kind. I am glad Nurse is staying for some time, sleeping here and cooking for me.

The two who bought this house are out so much I hardly see them. I do not yet know if I can stay here but I hope to be able to do so; I have paid the rent for the next three months. My nephew Robert is coming tomorrow, Sunday, to talk things over. He is a business man and very kind. I see him about once a year.

My family is spread over England and the Colonies but the girls come sometimes. They are quite nice but our lives are very different. I won't go to them as they have different tastes and I can't play cards very well; it would be an infliction on them to have an aged aunt. Here, there are many nice folk who knew Clare and the Minister and his wife are very, very kind. They have invited me to go to them for a time and included James in the invitation but I know it would be a little trouble to them; they are not well off. I will try to get someone who wants rooms; don't you think that would be the best plan?

I had to leave off from this letter as Nurse came in with a very nice dinner she had cooked. It was a chicken from you and was delicious. I was so sorry Clare could not eat it some time back but she would not allow that as she could only take gravy, which she had from many of your gifts.

You will understand me when I say I am glad she went first; she could not have stood the loss as well as I can do. What it means to me I am sure you know; 60 years of solid friendship is a long time but I am sure we shall meet again. Besides, I feel that she is with me now, sitting in the chair opposite to me and nursing James. Forgive this rather mixed up letter; Nurse is a little chatty. With my warmest love, to which I join Clare's, as she would wish.
Yours Always, Emilie.

Dear Angelique,

These touching little notes are Emilie's saddest letters and from their brevity we can grasp the grief she must be suffering; a sixty year friendship is indeed long. I am so immersed in Emilie's life I find it impossible not to be moved by her story, as it unfolds in the letters. Dear stern-looking Clare, who had such a loving heart that she preserved the illusion of her recovering, for Emilie's sake, meanwhile making plans for her own funeral and smoothing the way ahead in

practical matters, to help her not very practical friend. I am not going
to link news from the outside world or my own life to Emilie for the
time being; I will leave her to tell her own story for now.
Love from Victoria

Lavender Cottage.   April 10th 1952.

My Dear Friends and Cousins,

Your wire and Beatrice's letter helped me so much; it is difficult to
thank you enough. The people around here are very kind but cannot
give one the same feeling as your communication did, with such
sympathy and understanding. I felt they were my own words; you will
know what I mean.

I was glad to see my nephew on Sunday; I felt that I had never known
him before. He expressed his wish to do all he could. We hardly met
for 18 years and I regarded him as a business man and nothing more.
He was good to his mother so I ought to have judged him more fairly.
He and Clare's nephew have taken all business off my hands, which is
a great relief. I am very useless when it comes to figures. Clare did all
the household accounts; I wish you could have seen her account books,
every item entered and all in perfect order, mine as well as hers.

I shall have to leave here and will not regret it, except for the front
garden, where Clare worked when she was well; it used to be a lovely
sight. The minister will try to find me a suitable place but I am staying
here for at least three months as I have to see to Clare's clothes, etc. I
do wish that I could send you something Clare made. There is a mirror,
I think copper, hammered out by her. I keep looking at it but I don't
suppose I could post it, it is very heavy, though not large. Her other
things are heavier, carved wood. She was never good at needlework
but enjoyed carving. If you could think of anything you would like I
will be glad. There is no jewellery. I fear we parted with all that. Clare
kept only a little ring, her mother's I think and I squandered mine to
buy books that I wanted.

Please forgive writing and expression; the nurse and char lady are holding a brisk conversation. The nurse is to stay on for a time doing everything for me so I am well looked after. She is now making cigarettes and the other lady is cleaning up so I am well cared for. Your kindness and thoughts have made a hard time easier.

My warmest love to you, Emilie

Lavender Cottage. April 25th 1952.

My Dear Cousins,

I am so overwhelmed by your kindness I don't know how to write. Nurse keeps on at me; 'Why don't you sit down and keep still? You will make your head ache!' I said: 'It's worth many headaches to think of such kindness!'

I am so glad I shall now be able to repay her somehow for what she has done. She does not want to take anything and says she will stay until I am settled, either here or in a nice place. She knows how things are and that the people here are eager for me to go so that they may sell the house for a large sum. They cannot turn me out owing to the lease. Nurse said: 'Now, you can look round and find a place where you can take Miss Marriott's furniture and feel better'. Well, as I said, it is not easy to thank you adequately but I hope that you will understand how I feel about it.

You will be glad to hear that my nephew and Clare's have been kind in settling money matters, though probate will not be fixed for some months. They say I will have enough, with what Clare left me and my own money, to be comfortable, if, "I don't throw my money away!" The nephews want me to move as these people, they tell me, charge an exorbitant rent. This cannot be modified now as it was agreed by Clare and myself at the first; the mistake of not getting proper advice. Clare's nephew was in Venezuela at the time and as I had not seen my nephew for 18 years we had no one to advise us and were so anxious to stay here.

1952

Since Miss Lake died, my nephew has been very kind; he paid half of my rent and has continued to do so for two years. I hope to release him from that though he does not want me to do it. He feels I ought to leave Clare's nieces (there are two, who are not over well off) some of her money, which I intend to do. They are left £500 each, I understand. I am not young so shall invest what money I receive from Clare, so as to leave them what is right. I am sure you would approve of that.

Nurse is very anxious that I don't tell people around here about any money matters. Poor, dear Clare lent money to a neighbour two years ago without any acknowledgement and never received any repayment. So I promised Nurse to, "hold my tongue", as she phrased it. This is a very, "full of money" letter but I wanted you to know how things are. Clare would have been anxious for you to know that she had done her best for me after she had gone. I feel she is sending her love and thanks to you when I write. I had hoped that she would be here and well enough to enjoy life and friends a little longer but as it was it meant only pain for her.

With much love always, Emilie

Lavender Cottage.   June 5th 1952.

My Dear Cousins,

I have not written earlier, having no fresh news to give you and no special events to relate. I am still awaiting the settlement of money matters and having interviews with the lawyer, who is somewhat humorous; he says he hopes to finish sometime before Christmas. Meanwhile, and owing to your great kindness, Nurse and I are going on well. She has promised to stay until September, which gives me time to re-consider staying on here. I do want to do this as I feel Clar' Em'ly is still here and I don't think that I could bear a strange place. I am sure you will know she did all she could for me with regard to money and left everything in perfect order. They have not told me the full particulars as yet but my nephew thinks I shall find her provisions adequate.

1952

I made my will last week and have tried to act fairly towards Clare's relatives, though I must say that they do not wish me to consider them in any way. They are not rich but keep saying they have enough and the two girls are very pleased with the £500 they each get. The nephew and the niece are better off but I thought it only fair to remember them too. The lawyer laughs at me, like Nurse, he thinks I have a money spending capacity and there won't be much left when I have finished. Do forgive this business kind of letter but I feel I would like you to know how things are and it is advisable to have something to keep one's mind occupied, isn't it? It is a great relief to write to you; four of our old friends have gone here and the last, who is over 90, was very fond of Clar'Em'ly.

My nieces are very nice girls, we meet about once a year but as they all have husbands and children we have not very much in common. They are very kind and ask me to stay with them but I do not feel equal to the latest kind of whist every night! My nephew has been very good; for 18 years our only contact was exchanging Christmas cards but as soon as trouble came he wrote and has done all he could to arrange my staying here. The landlord is anxious to sell but cannot do that unless I leave and I am not anxious to go. What a long scrawl about my affairs! I am ashamed of it but it is good to be able to tell you about things, so I know you will excuse it.
Yours affectionately, Emilie

Lavender Cottage.   July 11th 1952

My dear Friends and Cousins,

I hope I have not been too long in writing but I was hoping to see whether affairs are settled so that I could give you some definite news but I am still in an indefinite state. I can say I will remain here for a year or more at any rate. I do not want to move and leave behind precious associations, as you may imagine. As you know, Clare has done all she could for me and I know she would wish me to remain. A few other matters here have still to be finished and I will let you know about these shortly. When Nurse goes in September a woman from our

Church will come. She can stay only until Easter but no doubt I can find someone else then.

I think about you both every night and wish you were nearer; people are very kind to me but I seem to have entered a new, strange life of which the best is missing. New friends cannot be made easily, can they? Four I have known for over fifty years have gone, one only remains and as she is over 90 she cannot travel from London and I am not allowed to go there, so there is no one who really belongs to me left. My nieces all have families and can only visit rarely so you will know how dear are your friendship and understanding; though you are a long way off you seem much closer than any here.

You will probably laugh but James is some comfort. Clare was also very fond of him. He is much injured at present, poor cat, having been sent to the vet again to have two teeth taken out. Nurse is very fond of him; I am sorry she has to go, she has been exceptionally kind. I have one or two little things I want to send to you but it is difficult, owing to postal regulations but I hope to get over there shortly. I should like a line when you have time; you are so understanding. I keep your wire and letter beside me.
With much love, Emilie.

Lavender Cottage.   August 14th 1952.

(For this letter Emilie has resorted once again to the elderly typewriter.)
Dearest Friends and Cousins,

This is an experiment and I fear a very unsuccessful one as this machine badly wants mending. It is nearly forty years old but I shall take it to town, when I can get there, and have it put right. Anyway, it is a little clearer than my writing. I was so pleased to have your letter and to hear your news. It is such a comfort to read your kind words; one does realise what real friendship is. I must amend your allusion to our climate. We really have had a 90 degree temperature and in the town the folks were really baked for a few weeks. We are 500 feet up so were spared the worst but we were actually forced into lighter clothes. Now we have rain, much needed, and the plants are reviving a little. For the holidaymakers' sakes we are glad to have had a finer summer than last.

I have not yet been allowed out alone but Nurse has taken me to town a few times and I have had the pleasure of taking her to dinner sometimes to save her from cooking. She is very kind as she will not accept her proper fee. I am using some of the money you more than kindly sent to buy her a dress and coat. I know she will welcome these and I know you will approve. Nurse leaves me next month as her sister is not over strong and will have to rest from nursing for some time. Nurse was to have taken me to London this week to see the friend of 91 whose own friend died a fortnight ago and who herself is in bad health. But my silly head refused to behave and the doctor said we had better wait a little while. My head is going on all right now and we shall be able to do the journey a little later. It is only a matter of two hours by car. Trains are more economical but the changing is so trying. I know that you would smile at a little journey like this with the wonderful distances you travel; I should have done so myself some years ago.

The lawyer has not finished with business affairs yet but I feel it will be all in order shortly. I will try and remain in this house, though the landlord would prefer me to leave but he cannot enforce it. The lawyer is of the opinion that I shall be able to stay here with which my nephew also agrees. I simply can't leave a place where Clare and I have been so long and where all the things around me are of her make and arrangement; I know you will both approve. I am sure the money will be sufficient so you are not to worry about that. You have been more than good to me and in other ways you have been so kind and such a comfort. I must end and repair the errors in this scrawl, for which forgive me.
Very Lovingly Yours, Emilie

1952

Lavender Cottage.   August 27th 1952.

My Very Dear Friends,

Just a short note to mention that I have sent you a tiny, 'trial' parcel in order to find out if I can send a later one. This sounds very Irish but no doubt you will understand. It is impossible to obtain any information here at the Post Office. I was told to write to London; from there I received 6 foolscap pages of directions which seemed to contradict each other but I did deduce that duty is not payable on items that are not valuable.

I want to send you something better of Clare's and mine but it is very trying if one's friends have to pay duty on trifles; why can't they just let me settle it? Please excuse writing; I am trying to dodge Nurse, who insists on an early bed. She is taking me to London tomorrow to see my last friend in England who is over 90 and very ill at present. There are many kind folk who come to see one but, well, you understand. We shall go by car as Nurse won't let me go by train, I shall lose her next month but there is another coming. Do forgive scrawl, Nurse is looking out of her door!
Much love from Emilie.

Lavender Cottage.   September 20th 1952.

My Dear Friends,

I have heard from Mr Humphries and I really don't know how to thank you, though I feel you ought not to have sent another gift to me after all your kindness this year.Indeed, my dears, I shall get on very well; I do admit to how splendidly I was able to settle all expenses and to recognise Nurse's goodness in remaining until this week, with a very much smaller charge than she usually makes.

Now the waiting for settlement is over and the lawyer says I need not sell Clare's dividend securities for a long time, so you see, dears, you must not worry about things on my behalf. You have been more kind to me than I can say in this sad time and it is so comforting to know you are so good to me. I agree that Clare's likeness is very good and represents her well. I do not know of any illustrious people in connection with her but all her relatives are remarkable for straight forward dealing and capability. Her brother-in-law is a first class civil servant and very ardent in politics. Her nephew was lately in two well known firms as head and is now under some government work.

Clare also had one niece, Kathleen Marriott, who has two really nice girls, one at home and the other managing a domestic science college. All are very good in writing to me and others come when they can. Clare's sister is far from well I regret to say but she is older than Clare was and probably will not outlive her for long. Excuse me not writing more at the moment but I want to post this letter before Nurse returns from shopping; she will not let me go out but I am quite fit to do so. Yours affectionately, Emilie.

Dear Angelique,

As we might have expected, Clare has left Emilie in a financially secure position but she is still full of uncertainty and anxiety about the future security of her home.

With reference to the "tiny trial parcel" Wendy sent me this email; "Have I ever told you that I have a book, Longfellow's Poetical Works, inscribed: "To Robert Crane Xmas 1887, from his beloved wife and daughter." I can't say for sure, but it does look like Emilie's writing. I'm trying to match it up with her writing in the first letter we have from her dated 1890. You know she was always trying to think of something to send Auntie Marion in the way of books that might be of interest. I think she may have sent this one, as we found it after my aunt died".

Like Emilie, I was undergoing my first experience of accommodation problems. The couple who employed my parents had decided to give up farming and buy a house with large gardens, just outside Lewes, Sussex. My father and mother were happy to accept the move and to continue as gardener/handyman and cook/housekeeper for their employers. They were also pleased to put some distance between myself and John, as they still did not approve of our relationship. They did not take into account my wilful streak. I refused to go with them and many weeks of arguments resulted in my getting my way. I was nearly eighteen.

With my parents' grudging consent, and after some difficulty, I found a room with a maiden lady in the Old Town part of Hastings, she provided three meals a day and I did my own washing and ironing. For bed and board I paid 21/-(£1.05p) per week. I was earning only 30/- (£1.50p) per week so I had very little money for necessities. My landlady was a Miss Smith and now I think about it she was rather like Emilie, both to look at and in her sense of humour. Miss Smith had been an Old Town child and spoke of attending a school there, in which children had to sit in galleried seats and she, as a four year-old, was seated in the topmost row. Nervous and shy, she was afraid to ask to go to the lavatory so wet her drawers and watched the stream make its way slowly down the steps to gather in a damning pool on the dusty classroom floor. She eventually became a dress-maker, working from her home. She told me that one afternoon, whilst doing a fitting on a rather portly lady, she felt an overwhelming urge to smack the plump backside that was presented to her face, as she knelt to adjust the hem of the dress. She succumbed to temptation! The startled client did not utter a word!

Hastings was still enjoying the status of a popular holiday resort. Early in the year the government had reduced the spending allowance for foreign travel and this restriction encouraged holidays at home. In August of 1952, an Old Town Preservation Society was proposed, this came too late to save many historic buildings but there can be no doubt of how important their work has been subsequently in saving much valuable architecture. The housing shortage in Hastings was being dealt with by the construction of council housing estates throughout the town and in August the government consented to people buying council houses. October saw the end of tea rationing but meat was still rationed. The President of the local branch of the Meat Traders' Association said to the 130 assembled members, at their annual dinner at the Royal Victoria Hotel, "Let us all hope that the day is not too far distant, when the task of the butchers will not be a misery of excuses and explanations, but a pleasure and a contribution to the well-being of British family life." He was referring to the meagre rationing system still in place six years after the official end of the Second World War.

There now follows a long gap in Emilie's correspondence; her first two letters of 1953 indicate that she is confused about the timing of events. Love from Victoria

1953

Lavender Cottage.   January 26th 1953.

Dear Marion and Beatrice,

I seem to have been a long time before writing but it was not for want of will, only a slight return of sickness, which has now passed. Did I thank you for sending the wire? I fear not and it was so kind of you. Did I tell you the kind next door habitant sent us in some chicken to help things seem Christmassy? I expect I did but my memory is not bright at present. The poor lady to whom I promised a Christmas dinner could not have eaten it; she was taken to hospital on Christmas Eve and is still there. The other neighbour who would have also partaken sent a letter of sympathy and took the will for the deed.

I hope, dears that you are both keeping well; the weather here is afflicting everyone, most of the folks are complaining of 'flu or bad colds. It is not possible to go out much but I did have two pleasant days last week, the first since before last Christmas. I was able to have lunch out and enjoyed the change in seeing a friend who knew Clare well. I wonder whether you will think I am imposing on your kindness if I ask if you have any used stamps you don't want. The canon, my neighbour, is interested in these and wants me to continue collecting these as I used to do. He thinks it would be better than reading as my eyes are bad. I began to collect them years back and have a small number still but nothing of any value. The canon thinks it will occupy my mind as I can't get out often.

I have made no arrangements to move so far and Robert, my nephew, does not wish me to do this for some time. I do not see him often as he has his London business but he will always write and advise me if there is need. The canon and his wife have promised to look out for a suitable place if it becomes necessary. They are moving out next month, I am sorry to say, as this neighbourhood is too far from the town for them. They have been so kind, though I do not belong to their church. However, there is plenty of time for me to make changes. My very best love to you both and hope to hear from you when you have time, telling me you are keeping well and getting nice weather or having snow. Do take care of yourselves.
Yours affectionately, Emilie,

1953

February 23rd 1953.

Dear and Kindest of Friends,

It is difficult to write when words seem inadequate to convey all one feels. I can only say that owing to your loving message, which arrived last week, Christmas was full of happy thoughts. I had re-experienced sorrowful memories of last Christmas and the feeling there was no one there who could grasp them, but your message came with assurance that two understood and joined in with wonderful sympathy. That was sufficient gift, I assure you, without the added gift that came this morning. My dears, it is so good of you, well, I can't say enough or adequately. You will smile when I tell you that I was like a child and I shouted to my new help: "Mrs Cole, we will go out to lunch tomorrow and I will get you that new hat you have been longing for!" She really has been kind and I wanted to get her something she has been longing for (please excuse repetition; I am still a little shaky).

Please don't think dears that I am in need of anything necessary, you are not to worry about that. The lawyer tells me there is enough to last for some time to come. The joy of getting things above the usual necessities is very great. I can hear Clare saying, "You always did like buying little extras". That was so true in my case. Did I tell you in my last that the threatened pneumonia did not arrive? The doctor says that it will not trouble me, now that the worst weather is over. I keep wondering what kind of winter you are having; here the worst seems to be over. Hastings has been spared the floods that have troubled the East and Yorkshire coasts, together with the Dutch provinces. I always wonder how our southern coast escapes; it is very low-lying in parts. I do trust that you escape all that and hope you never have the bitter cold with which Guelph favoured us when we were there.

Mrs Cole has said that if I want the postman to take that letter in the morning I had better leave off writing. For your sakes I think it might be as well to stop, though I feel I could go on for ever. I must just add that James, the cat, ought to send his love for his share in the food and visits from the vet. He is 17 (James I mean) and is threatened with being put away but I am trying to keep him as long as possible; Clare

was very fond of him. Goodbye for a little while and my love and every good and heartfelt wish to you two dears. Oh dear, what a badly written letter!
Emilie

Dear Angelique,

You see what I mean about Emilie's confusion, so her reference to the floods was unexpected. It was on February 3rd that hurricane force winds, together with high tides, visited disaster on Britain's east coast. In the floods that followed at least 280 people were drowned and thousands made homeless. In Holland, dykes burst and over 1,000 were drowned. Hastings rallied to help the UK east coast flood victims with money, clothing and necessities and the town's Women's Royal Voluntary Service contributed clothing and blankets. In the middle of the catastrophe, sweet rationing ended for the second time.

By spring 1953 I had become accustomed to living in lodgings. Twice a month John took me to Lewes for the weekend to visit my parents and we stayed overnight with them, in the servants' quarters of their employer's Regency house. In deference to my parents' anxieties, John had sold his smart, sports motor bike and bought something more mundane, complete with a sidecar, which was supposedly safer but much duller transport for me. During the winter journeys to Lewes John would tuck me up in the sidecar with blankets and a hot water bottle, while he froze outside.

My job as a "well spoken shop girl" continued. I was promoted to first sales in haberdashery, which meant I had the first pick of customers, thus more of the modest commission, plus an increase in my week's pay to 34 shillings. Shop girls were considered to be very low in the 50's social pecking order and many customers treated us accordingly. The senior staff behaved as if they were running a reform school; there were rigid rules concerning dress (black only) and behaviour, even down to the way the shop assistants spoke to each other. A haughty, elegant lady floor walker toured all departments to keep an eye on our conduct and to make sure we were not slouching or sitting down. Incredible, isn't it? Who would tolerate that these days?
Love from Victoria

1953

Lavender Cottage.   April 25th 1953.

My Dear Friends,

Please forgive my not writing earlier but I have had a nasty return of the October illness. However, it is improving now and the weather is much warmer. I hope you are both keeping well in spite of the cold; I should be so glad of a line to hear. I am going to beg something and I hope you won't mind. The person who looks after me can't be made to understand I need paper handkerchiefs, not bits of tissue that last just a moment. She has bought me boxes of these and they are gone in a day. You sent me some nice large ones last year and they were so nice.

I feel I ought not to ask, after all you have done for me, but if it is possible to send a few, they would be a boon. I am not in need of anything else; I can tell you that there is enough money to keep me for some years and to leave enough for Clare's relatives and mine so please, don't worry about that. It would not be right for your money to go to a stranger. Forgive me for talking about money won't you? If the time ever came when I needed any I would let you know.

I have not made any arrangements about leaving here. I may have to do so later, as it is difficult to get "helps" at this distance from town. Two of mine come alternately and are quite kind but one can't help missing Clare. I have only one old friend left who is infirm and 90 years old; she is in London so we don't meet often. This letter sound rather like a wail but really, dears, I have much to be thankful for and most especially for your friendships and remembrances. The country is full of the coming coronation but I do not contemplate journeying to London.
Yours affectionately, Emilie.

Dear Angelique,

I think we can grasp Emilie's absent mindedness by the fact that she does not mention the death, in her sleep on 25th March, of Queen

Mary; she was the grandmother of the young Queen Elizabeth. What a sad coincidence that the Queen suffered the loss of her mother at a similar interval from her Golden Jubilee. Here is a quote about Queen Mary from one of my research sources. "She was a tall regal figure...for 50 years her dress never changed; her jewelled toque sat on top of tightly packed curls and there was always the same style of coat". The Queen Mother and now Queen Elizabeth adopted a way of dressing that is almost a uniform, the same style of garment, in a wide variety of colours and fabrics. How supremely sensible!
Love from Victoria

Lavender Cottage.   May 31st 1953.

Dear Marion and Beatrice,

Very many thanks for your kind letter and news. It would have been lovely to see you both but I think that you are wise to be absent at this time. The mobs of folk who have come and are coming, to England are appalling; half a million are already camped out on pavements and in parks, with blankets and two days' food. The newspaper reckoned that two million people will see the procession or rather, try to see it. No doubt the people coming from abroad will be staying on for some time afterwards and so we cannot look forward to peace just yet.

I do hope that your cold is better; I was glad to hear that you could have meals out of doors and your garden sounds very pleasing. Our new people are very quiet, the man is a gardener, having his own nursery; we may hope to be given a modicum of vegetables. Unfortunately, our part of the house is sold to his or her sister, not an attractive person, who is anxious to come here.

Of course, we need not move, being protected by the agreement but it makes thing a little uncomfortable. However, I cannot move until autumn and not then if I cannot find a suitable place. My nephew may pay me a visit after the coronation is done with; he is a good adviser. My difficulty here is to get help; the present one, naturally, wants her holidays and people who might come, object to the distance from town. However, I must not bother you with these things; they will sort themselves out in time.

I note you have had a lot of rain, hence, your cold! We have had too little but it rather looks as if we are going to make up, it's very cloudy at present; it will be bad for the outdoor folk. Please forgive the writing; I cannot have stronger glasses, or so the oculist tells me and the present ones are bad in dull weather. I do wish I could see you but I fear even television would not be very successful.
With very much love to you both, Emilie.

Dear Angelique,

As I write we are celebrating Queen Elizabeth's Golden Jubilee and here is Emilie writing about the coronation; her first paragraph could easily have been written about the recent events. In June 2002 the British rallied in their millions to celebrate the Golden Jubilee, a four day party, enhanced by technology that would have been beyond Emilie's wildest imaginings..

In 1953, relentless rain drizzled down all over the country on Coronation Day. The Hastings and St Leonards Observer printed the good old cliché, "un-dampened by rain and wind" when describing the day's festivities in the town. There were 14 street parties, tree-planting ceremonies, bonfires and fireworks. Two Royal Navy destroyers, Agincourt and Corunna, were anchored off Hastings. The fishermen built a traditional, celebratory arch in the Old Town and people all over the town partied till the small hours. I found an account of the Hastings' St George's Road coronation street party: "Ninety children enjoyed a tea of cheese and meat sandwiches (I bet it was Spam) fancy and fruit cake, lemonade and, as a special treat, ice cream." It was raining so the party was held in the nearby Mendem Hall; every child went home with a souvenir.

Millions of people all over the world saw the coronation, live, on television. I went to Guestling Village Church with John and we saw the coronation on a screen, set up in front of the altar, and we participated in the service with hymns and prayers; I was moved by the

solemnity of the occasion and all the glorious pomp and military precision. I was also delighted by the procession and loved Queen Salote of Tonga, a powerfully built woman, who smiled and waved throughout the parade, as her open coach filled with rainwater. In the late afternoon John suggested we went to London by train. On arrival, we struggled down the crowded and wonderfully decorated Mall, until we were squashed against the Buckingham Palace railings. To the crowd's chant of, "We want the Queen "she appeared on the balcony; a tiny, robed figure but even at that distance I could see the flash of the jewels in the crown. The press of people became frightening and I lost my hold on John's hand and was being pushed down, under the feet of the crowd. My terrified shrieks brought him to my rescue, what a dramatic end to the day. I do hope Emilie was able to follow the ceremony on her wireless; the coronation music was beautiful, I am sure she would have enjoyed it.
Love from Victoria,

Lavender Cottage.   September 14th 1953

Tel. Hastings 51101.

My Dear Friends,

It seems a long time since I have written to you but my thoughts have gone out to you all along. My news would have been very samey, mainly an account of fresh people coming to do the daily work and to sleep at night, nothing very exciting. Certainly their tastes in cooking provide a sense of curiosity; one never knows what eatables will appear on the table and whether they would, in fact, be eatable.

Not that I worry about that, usually, I am more interested in my cat's appetite. He is most particular and food must be varied to meet his requirements. He is 17-18 years so must be forgiven fussiness. What he won't eat is bestowed on a stray cat that comes here twice a day for food; he is not particular.

I think I told you about the new tenants who have bought the house. They are quite nice and kindly and I should like to stay with them but unfortunately, half the house is to be occupied by their brother and sister and they are anxious to take up residence.

They cannot turn me out as my lease has some years to run and I need not leave. They are nice about it but I fear it is hard on them. My nephew, who looks after my interests, is against my moving and indeed it is difficult to know where to go, especially as people do not want furniture and I dread a new place. But I don't grumble; it's only that one feel so lonely without real friends; I know you will understand. It would be lovely if you were nearer but it is good to know you are thinking of me and understand how I feel.

One of my nieces came and stayed a week. She was very nice and kind but of course she has to come from London every time. Still, it was good to see her as one could go about a little with her. Dear oh dear, this sounds a very discontented epistle, doesn't it? You must forgive me but I know you understand how one feels; very lonesome at times, but I always think of you two and I am so glad to be able to write to you.
My love to you both, Emilie.

Lavender Cottage.   November 16th 1953.

My Dear Friends,

You will think that I am very slack in writing but there is nothing new to tell you. Things go on in the same way, the only changes being a little variation in the people who come to look after me; there have been five on and off this year and one was able to come for a fortnight. It does make a change anyway. I am hoping to have a visit from my niece at Christmas; she is a cheerful person in spite of losing two husbands and not being left well off. She has a gift for bullying the trade's people if they don't obey orders, which is most amusing. The present lady is going to friends for Christmas for one week; last year she had to remain with me. That was the sorrowful occasion when your lovely present was grabbed by the officials, who said that despatches of this kind were forbidden. I must confess this statement was taken sceptically!

The people who have bought this house are quite nice but of course are anxious to have their relatives here, an event difficult to bring about. I cannot see yet how to gratify them; I do want to keep some of the furniture, especially that which belonged to Clare. I wish for a place that would give some nursing but not a 'nursing home'. It is not easy; nearly all houses are turned into flats or guest houses, where one's furniture is not allowed. Do forgive me for bothering you with all these uninteresting particulars but it is a relief, as kind as other people are, they can't take an interest in other folks' affairs. I have been trying to find a nice book to send you; it is difficult as I can't get to town unless escorted and other people don't want to lose time while one examines books. I found one but I expect that you have read it. I have a good many of my own books and wish some would be useful to you but it is difficult to select these. Bless you both and may Christmas be a happy one for you.

Yours affectionately, Emilie

Lavender Cottage.   November 24th 1953

My Dear Friends,

I have been trying to get something to send to you. But not being able to go to town without an escort it is so difficult to get some time to look at any thing. I wanted some nice books but what I saw was not to my liking. The other is not new but Clare was very fond of it, though you must know it by heart. It is such an old one but I wanted you to have it. I shall look round when my help comes at Christmas; she doesn't mind looking at books.

I was invited to my nephew in London but I don't feel quite up to it just now. I hope you get the cards, though they, too, are not what I wished. My present help is going for a holiday but she returns later. This is not a letter really, only an explanation of my failure to send a nice book and to repeat my love and good wishes for your happy time at Christmas. I wish I could see you and give my wishes in person but my very best thoughts are all that can reach you.

With Much Love, Emilie.

1953

Dear Angelique,

*How sad it is to see Emilie's life closing in; these days there would be
so much that could be done for her to keep her in touch with life. She
really is the least self-pitying person I have met and always thinking of
others. As 1953 drew to a close, austerity was loosening its grip, as if
the coronation had created a watershed. The nation's accommodation
problem improved radically, in the month of October alone over
30,000 houses were built and on November 5th it was announced all
rationing would end in 1954.*
*I was nineteen in November and John asked me to marry him. I said,
'Yes'.*
Love from Victoria.

1954

Lavender Cottage.   Jan 1st 1954.

Dear Marion and Beatrice,

I can't think of anything but your kindest of messages and those lovely flowers. They were wonderful and I knew in a moment from whom they came; the most beautiful things! Everyone who has seen them has exclaimed and others came in to share their beauty. I don't know who brought them in so I was not able to thank him or her but the senders were obvious, long before I saw the message on them.

I do thank you both over and over again; they were just lovely things and made Christmas so real. Your messages, too, added to my realisation that it was a real Christmas and that the kindest of people were sending lovely thoughts to me. It was a real Christmas in every way after that beginning. Clare's nieces and their father sent a car from their home, about 18 miles away, and took me to spend the day with them; they are such kind people; you would like them very much . Mrs Cole had gone on Thursday and I could not get a substitute for sleeping but the new folks here are very nice and left the doors of their rooms open all night to assure me that they would come if I became too nervous. There was no need as James and I had good nights.

On Saturday and Sunday I went over to the good lady who had kindly bought me a turkey and she cooked it very well. It was a big one and it lasted us until Sunday and Monday, if we felt like it. It was Mrs Todd, the person to whom you sent the parrot food, which she has never forgotten. Unfortunately, she is not well off; she has had to give up keeping the chickens, perhaps it is just as well, as she is getting old. The new people are very nice but of course they are anxious to have their brother, aged 90, and sister with them. I would willingly stay in two rooms, though it would be rather constricted; moving is such a bother. My help would have to go. I send you my warmest love and thanks for all your kindness; it has made a lovely Christmas for me. Emilie.

1954

Lavender Cottage.   No date, envelope postmarked 4th January
1954.

My Dear Kind Friends,

Please forgive this paper. I cannot get to the town to obtain the usual ones and the people up here can supply only the usual thick stuff. I was delighted to have your letter with all its news and am glad the magazine was of some use. I did not want to send the last one as I didn't consider The Lady to be very respectable. But my help, Mrs Cole, posted it off with an added picture before I could stop it. Mrs Cole has now gone on holiday and I had much difficulty in obtaining another help. We are so far from the town that substitutes are hard to find. However, I now have a Cambridge girl who is on holiday; she is quite nice but not the help Mrs Cole was. I am so glad you had a good holiday; you are such dears and deserve all the best. I, too, wish Canada was nearer. One cannot but feel cut off without real friends near. Yesterday, I was very extravagant. I went to see my oldest friend in London; she is over 90 and has had two strokes. She has a bad leg and never gets out; she was so pleased to see me; a kind person, Edith Lake's sister, came with me. We had a car but I am a little shaky and the two and a half hour drive was very tiring. I was very glad I went but it may be the last time I see her; she is my last friend in England.

A very kind friend died three weeks ago; I went to the funeral service at Maidstone but could not get to Charing where Clare, Edith Lake and two other friends lie. Oh dear, what a gloomy epistle! But I am not depressed please don't think it; I can't be when I have such lovely friends to whom I can write. My nephew is coming to see me this afternoon. He comes about once a year and gives good advice, which his aunt does not always follow! (There is terrible amount of repetition in this epistle, do excuse it. My head is usually rather stupid in the morning). I can just see you having your meals in the porch.
LATER
At that point my nephew and his wife arrived so my writing was interrupted. They were both very kind but he was very business-like and made me render information for my accounts, pulling me up on some things, all for my good, of course! It is necessary for him to check my accounts; I am so bad at figures. The cat insists on being

nursed, hence this bad handwriting. He is 17 this month but he has a lion's appetite. I am ashamed of my writing and have half a mind to get my typewriter mended though I may not be able to type without looking. It would save the eyes but the recipient of my letter might not be able to read it.

Yours affectionately, Emilie.

Dear Angelique,

In January 1954, both Emilie and I had little reason to be interested in the doings of Hastings or the wider world; she was coping with the loss of friends, increasing disability and concerns about her home and I was pre-occupied with my forthcoming marriage.

I have been unable to trace descendents of the good Mrs Cole; I even resorted to the desperate measure of phoning the Coles listed in the local telephone directory, with no luck. I also did a broadcast appeal on local radio for relatives or anyone who might have remembered the three ladies at Lavender Cottage; I began to wonder where this quest for Miss Emilie Crane's history would lead me. The only response to the radio appeal was from a retired housing officer who phoned me to suggest I tried residences for the elderly. A daunting task, there are so many in Hastings and St Leonards.
Love from Victoria.

Lavender Cottage.   March 14th 1954.

My Dear Friends,

It seems a long time since I wrote but it has been, and still is, a brisk time getting ready for the new people to come in, which they expect to do on the 24th. They have allowed me to keep two rooms so we have been disposing of beds and furniture; having to give most of it away as people don't want beds of the old pattern nowadays. I do not mind furniture so much; it is my books I dislike parting with. Still, I have managed to keep two good sized cases of the best. I know you would sympathise with that. The new people are relatives of those here already; one is an old man of over 90 and the other his niece, who seems quite amiable but has rather a terrible voice. She has two cats and a dog. All this means getting rid of Mrs Cole, who has been with me for some months. She regrets leaving but there is no room for her and the new person promises to look after me.

Please excuse this paper; I managed to upset the inkstand and hadn't another cover to replace it. I hope the postman won't object. One cannot buy these papers except in the town. I do object to begging but if you could send me a small piece of cheese I should be so glad. We get a kind of Dutch cheese here. They say the food will be improved soon. If you can't do it, don't mind saying so. You may not be allowed to send things but I fancy they are not so strict now. My "help", who comes to tidy up, says her daughter, in London Ontario, sends some food now and then. Please don't do it if it's a bother and do forgive me for asking and this badly written letter. Apologies for this scribble and heaps of love to you both.
Emilie

Lavender Cottage. May 5th 1954

My Dear Friends,

At the moment people are revelling in real cheese! It arrived this morning and had to be sampled as soon as possible. It's delicious, so different from the stuff we get here; you were too good to send such a noble amount. I had given up on cheese as ours is no good and it's a real treat. I am going to take two little lots out tomorrow to rejoice two more neighbours.

I have nothing fresh to record; the old gentleman of 95 is still going strong and his niece tries to look after us both. Fortunately, I have kept fairly well since Christmas and do not require much waiting on. The weather has been very cold but as I can get out but little it does not worry me much; it is difficult to walk and cars are not very reasonable.

I have not been able to go to church as it is so far off; anyway it is useless going when one cannot hear a word of anything. Still, the minister comes in fairly often and people look in here when not too busy. I have a chat with the old gentleman every evening but cannot read to him as my eyes are so poor.

My friend in London writes when she can but she is 94 and lives with a delusion that I never write to her! I should like to go and see her but cannot manage it at present. I wish you wanted some books; I have so many and cannot bear to part with them to strangers. Anyway, I don't suppose they would wish for them. It is a pity as they are so good. This is a poor epistle but my news is always the same.

I send my very, very best love and warmest thoughts and thanks.
Emilie.

Dear Angelique,

Emilie's craving for cheese makes me think of Ben Gunn in Treasure Island! How sorry I feel for her in the sameness of her days.

I wonder what she means by "beds of the old pattern that nobody wants nowadays"; probably these are the very beds, with breath-taking price tags, occasionally seen in Hastings' antique shops today. May 1st 1954 had been our wedding day; a very modest affair in financial terms, not only because my parents were hard up but because that was what we both wanted. We were married at St Pancras Catholic Church, Lewes (I recall I mis-spelled it Pancreas on the invitations!) We had a two-day honeymoon at a grand hotel in Chichester, opposite the cathedral and returned to live in two rooms, with shared bathroom, probably less living space than Emilie, in what had been a farmhouse in Georgian times, in Old London Road, Hastings.

Love from Victoria.

1954

Lavender Cottage.   July 26th 1954

Dear Marion and Beatrice,

This is only a note as I wished to ask whether you would not prefer Everybody's and another paper sent. This one must be growing tedious and there are several other publications now. That is really the gist of my note as I have no special news except that I fear my cat must go; he is about 18 and mostly occupied by sleep. I shall miss him very much as he is all that is left of the old times, excepting my friend of 94 and she is getting very strange nowadays.

I must tell you again how the cheese was enjoyed by many around; I have had nothing to come near it in these parts. I am not enjoying things very much, though the new people are kind enough; the old gentleman is most talkative but one cannot understand any of his remarks. I do so wish I could hear your voices.
Very much love to you both-always.
Yours Emilie, or Ethel, whichever you prefer.

Lavender Cottage.   No date. Letter postmarked 1st September
1954.

My Dear Friends,

I have been hoping for a long time to get a letter from you and had I not received your kind messages and flowers and later the very nice cheese, I would have thought you were ill or away. Do send a word if you can, it is so lonely here without a word from friends. People are very kind but there is no one friend except in London; she is over 90 and lame. It is too far for nieces to come and they all have their own occupations and I cannot get to London but rarely.
Do drop a line if you can if it's only to say you are well.
With much love,
Emilie.

1954

Lavender Cottage.   No date. Letter postmarked 15th September 1954.

My Very Dear Friends,

I ought to have known something was wrong and never to have sent a silly letter. I am so sorry I got excited and boxed my own ears for it. What a terrible and worrying time for you both, you dears. I ought to have known better than to send stupid letters and how good of you to write so quickly. Oh! I am so glad you are really better, though I expect you exaggerate in that. Poor Marion too! These are times when one wishes for the wings of a dove. If it hadn't meant weeks to get to you I guess I would have tried it. I asked someone who had come over but she came by the quick way and the money wasn't big enough and it would have been a nuisance to you.

Do excuse this badly written and excitable letter; you can guess by it how glad I am. Though it means a lot of care and much tiredness for Marion but I know that won't worry her. Don't either of you write for a long time. I shall be all right now and if I send lots of letters don't think about answers. I am all right, requiring only a few extra legs but there is no rheumatism or anything. The new person who has bought this part of the house is not bad but I will tell you all about it when I write next. This is a stupid kind of letter but you will understand; it is because I am so glad. I hope to find a better paper now. Heaps of love to you both; excuse writing and everything.
Yours, with heaps of love.
Oh! I said that already but I can't repeat it too often.
To both my warmest love and wishes.
Emilie,

Dear Angelique,

In this letter Emilie's handwriting is deteriorating, possibly due to her failing eyesight. The very real distress she is expressing is probably the cause of the confusion in her narrative. How I feel for her loneliness.
Love from Victoria

1954

Lavender Cottage.　　　Postmarked 1st November 1954.

My Very Dear Friends,

Your letter was most welcome and I was glad to hear there was a little improvement. I felt there must be some to enable you to write yourself. It has been a very long illness and both of you must be worn out. I feel so useless on these occasions; why cannot one fly like the birds?

I tried to get to the town to see what one could do by messages; my book said that they could be sent by various methods and one could really speak to friends, if only for two or three minutes but my stupid head could not get to the proper place and I had to put aside this method. I could not get the correct details so had to go back to letters. I wonder, whether I can send the books? I have so many but they may not be suitable and I can't get particulars of details in this place so I might send too many, or vice versa, and so plunge you into expense. It is getting so near Xmas and I wish to send something suitable.

I think I shall have to move from here as it is too far from the town, I hope to be able to find something. It is not very comfortable here though the woman is very kind. The relatives are very good in writing but are too far away. The doctor says I must keep in Hastings so I must find a more convenient place. There is nothing wrong but one's silly legs, which will not walk. But then I must not talk about myself; I would give so much for a sight of you both. Please forgive a limited and somewhat un-fluent epistle.
I will write again to tell you all that happens, especially if any change occurs. My very loving words to you both.
Yours Always, Emilie.

Lavender Cottage.　　　Post marked 28th December 1954

My Dear Friends,

Fondest love to you. Just a little note to send my love and to say that all is well with me except that the long threatening slight loss of words has attacked me and I feel I must just warn you- unpleasant but not more serious. My age has made this natural. I shall be able to write better after a little-don't worry about it.

I do so hope you are getting on well, bless you both and I hope you had the messages in time and the books. The cards were not good but the best other people could get. You can see my writing will improve soon. The flowers are so really just like you both. I will write as soon as I can and send you both more love than I can express on this. Love to the little dog.
With much love, Emilie.

Dear Angelique,

Trust Emile to make little of her deteriorating health and living conditions. One suspects there is a lot more going on in Lavender Cottage than she reveals.

During our first married Christmas I did not see my parents. A misunderstanding with them over a joint, family summer holiday booking had caused a rift. I felt wretched as I was also feeling unwell and confused, often very tearful, with bouts of nausea and vertigo, I even fainted in church. How ignorant can one be? I was, of course, pregnant!
Love from Victoria.

1955

Lavender Cottage.   Sunday 13th February 1955.

Dear Marion and Beatrice,

I fear this will be a stupid letter as I am feeling very dense and unable to use proper words. This took place in the Christmas time when I was trying to send greetings to everyone and found I had to fall back on someone else to write them. It is strange that my writing has returned but the words will not. Well, my best of friends, I can but send you my love and hope that all will be well with you and that you are going on well with your return to health and that all time to come will be very happy. The little dog, too, must have my message of love. I do miss my own too.

We are having changes here; the people who had the other half of the house were cheated by one of the owners and are obliged to move to an inferior place. The old uncle (95) and his daughter (niece?) stay on; she has the disadvantage of being unable to cook. My nephew sent me word that I was to move and go to their place at once, leaving the poor woman behind, with no one to help her. Being a coward, I said I would go then changed my mind and upset him very much. That does not trouble me for I have been in this house so long with Clare. I may have to move as the woman may not be able to pay the rent, so things are really in a muddle.

However, as I feel only in muddle myself it doesn't seem to matter much. I think I shall obtain new lodgers as the rooms next door are very nice, being those Clare built.
Well, my dears if you understand all this you will be very clever (which you are) but I told you my head was mixed!
I send you heaps of love and more. Take care of your dear selves.
Yours Always, Emilie

1955

Dear Angelique,

Emilie's message of love to the dog and her comment, "I miss my own too" must be a reference to the end of James' life. What a remarkable cat he was, living for almost eighteen years, no doubt that was down to the pampering and loving care from his mistresses. It is very difficult to discover exactly who owned the seperate parts of Lavender Cottage at this point; a 1953 street directory lists the property occupants as Miss E. E. Crane and Mr Frederick Tatt. Emilie is certainly confused about the situation. Her poor speech may have been a contributory factor to her family and co-occupant problems.

At this time, my mind too was in a state of confusion. I did not have my pregnancy medically confirmed until late January 1955. I was terrified at the thought of childbirth and motherhood and so postponed the visit to the doctor for as long as possible, as if that would have made any difference! The news about the baby was greeted on John's part by a rush of tenderness and by the rest of his family with delight. I was surprised by all this fuss at what was to me an unwelcome condition. In the fifties there was no formula for discussing one's fears and reservations about being pregnant, you were supposed to be overjoyed automatically!
Love from Victoria.

30, Laton Road,   Postmarked 28th March 1955
Hastings, England.

My Dears,

I am so sorry unable to write, I had a turnout with last woman and had to leave her. Present place very nice but it is a kind of guest house and I fear I want more attention and didn't know quite what to do and it's difficult to look about but don't worry something will come. Have taken one place but not fit. It needs more attention in my case. But don't worry it will turn up. Much love to your dear selves. E.

Bleaton Lodge Guest House,   Post marked 13th April
30 Laton Road,
Hastings
My Dear Friends,

I have not any cheerful news to give you and am very sorry to communicate anything which is not lively but I feel I must write. My move from the old place was somewhat stormy; the good lady and myself disagreed and I went hurriedly, finding refuge here and removing all my furniture before realising I had struck a guest house, where you are under supervision and do not go your own way! As I did not agree with the various orders, the inhabitants are not very fond of me and my limits are somewhat irritating. I must confess I was not over agreeable and find myself rather fed up with rules!

Of course I can leave but the alternatives are not prepossessing. Please excuse my writing, I have no proper pen and cannot go out to buy, minus an escort. I would go to my nephew Bob's place but he has given rooms and help to his own family and also the distance is so great. I went last Saturday but the expense too much to go often. I was interrupted by the head lady entering, so had to make polite remarks. But will write more. She is not a bad old thing but I can't stand being restricted. Much love to you both and I do hope you are keeping as well as you can. Let me have a line to say how you both are and excuse this scrawl; it's hard writing in semi-darkness,
Yours ever, heaps of love
Unsigned

Dear Angelique,
The condition of this letter gives an indication of Emilie's state of mind; it has crossings out and ink blots, so unlike her usual neat style. Records do not show if Bleaton House was a nursing home, it was listed in 1953 as being occupied by William Henry Newman and we learn later that the "head lady", to whom Emilie refers is Mrs Newman. The comment about rules does suggest an institution, rather than a guest house but one cannot be sure. In the 1950s "regulations" in guest houses were the norm. Just recently, 30 Laton Road came on

the market and I went to view it, explaining to the estate agent my particular interest. I found it had rather a sad atmosphere. It had been a nursing home until March 2002, when the owner had abandoned it, with the beds still tumbled and unmade. It is currently divided into single bedrooms, thirteen in all. I hope that there were fewer rooms in Emilie's day and that the multiple sleeping spaces are just modern, commercial expediency. I walked between the rooms and tried to imagine Emilie there. The house was Victorian family home, before it was sub-divided. The views from the rear, upper windows are of the treetops of Alexandra Park and, at the front, Blacklands Church. I was inside the house for less than 5 minutes; the agent was in a hurry so this is just an impression.
Love from Victoria

30 Laton Road.　　　Postmarked 25th April 1955.

My Dear Friends,

Thank you very much for your letter. I am so very sorry to hear of Beatrice's accident and send her my very best love and hope it will not be a very long and sad illness. How worrying for you both my dears and I shall rejoice when the news is of good progress. Your address to Bob is all right but I usually send letters, unless business ones, to Olive his daughter; she does enjoy them but at present she is changing her address and goes to her grandchild. The address has not come to me yet. But Mrs Sybil Milne, 62, Elmhurst Court, St Peter's Road, Croydon, will always get a reply. I will send on Olive's address as soon as I have it.

Anyway, all letters have to come to me and there is no prospect of my changing now. I have altered only once since I came from London, with Miss Marriott, even then was in my own place (The Ridge), which the woman bought. I really have not changed. I am afraid this is very badly written but I did want you to know I have been in one place ever since I left London and should not have left The Ridge, had I been treated fairly. The people at The Ridge all know it. I have been here seven weeks only and have no intention of moving, unless my own people want me, which they don't, having too many already. I am afraid this is a very vague letter but I hope you will be able to read it. My writing may improve! I hope Marion will get on well-much love to you both and a kiss for the dear little kitten.

Your loving Emilie

Dear Angelique,

This letter indicates Emilie's ever growing confusion, with spelling mistakes, alterations and muddled facts. We will never know the exact details of what finally went wrong at Lavender Cottage but the seeds of the problems were certainly sown in 1949 with Edith Lake's death. In trying to find the name of Emilie's Lavender Cottage antagonist I learned there was no street directory printed for 1954/55 but in 1956, a Miss Mann was the sole occupant of Lavender Cottage. Was she the 95 year old man's niece/daughter and the woman with whom Emile had the "turnout" and from whom she made the stormy and hurried departure?

Love from Victoria.

Undated letter from Miss Marion Ellis of Canada to Mrs Sybil Milne, written some time after April 25th 1955.

My Dear Mrs Milne,

My cousin, Emilie Crane, in Hastings, gave me your name and address, though my own name will be unfamiliar to you. Some years ago, my grandmother, Mrs Edward Neeve King, of London, Ontario, took me to see Miss Crane, who was her cousin; the late Robert Ewart Crane being Cousin Emilie's father and my grandmother's uncle.

Of late years I have corresponded with Cousin Emilie at Lavender Cottage and recently at the Bleaton Lodge Guest House, 30, Laton Road, Hastings. I have been distressed to know she has not been well and so I asked her to let me know the address of some relative with whom she corresponds and she gave me your name.

Of late we have exchanged letters frequently and enjoyed the friendship but when she is ill there is not a soul in Hastings from whom I can get any word of her. I had a letter from her this morning, in which her writing was rather confused, which made me fear she may not be so well. If you have any recent news of her I should be grateful if you would let me know how she is.
Sincerely,
(Miss) Marion Ellis

62, Elmhurst Court,
St Peter's Road,
Croydon Surrey.   14/6/55

Dear Miss Ellis,

I have refrained from answering your letter before because of our very serious postal strike. We have been asked to reduce our letter writing but I am hoping to hear some good news on the radio this evening, so will endeavour to mail this without delay. I must start this by saying I was most impressed to receive your letter; it was so nice to hear you have Auntie's interests at heart. By the way, are you aware that Miss Emilie Crane is my Aunt? She is a sister of my father who was Robert Ewart Crane.

I am afraid Auntie is far from well; her sight is very poor and she is ageing a lot. I receive many letters and phone calls from her which I fail to understand. I have made a few recent trips to try and urge her to come and live near us but this she would not do on any account. I think she is now being well cared for; her previous people she was with made her most unhappy. Auntie has always been a most generous lady and now she is a little simple. She is offering sums of money to many people, some are strangers, but all gladly accept her gifts. Her bank manager is most concerned about her account but I am powerless; she will not listen to my advice. I only hope she has sufficient to end her days in comfort as I am in no position to support her entirely.

A few weeks ago she had a sudden desire to spend a day with me so she hired a car to bring her 160 miles. I have now learned she paid the driver dearly. She also had a roll of banknotes on her and tried hard to get my son and myself to help ourselves. Needless to say, we declined, but many would have taken it from her. I will certainly keep you informed of Auntie's health, she was, and is, my favourite relative. She has retained her sense of humour and still enjoys her smoking.

Once again, I thank you for your kind enquires.

Sincerely yours.

Sybil Milne (Mrs)

This next is Emilie's final letter to Marion and Beatrice, post marked 27th May 1955 and sent from Bleaton House. Her handwriting is now cramped and difficult to read and the script rambles across the page unevenly, with many gaps and uncompleted sentences. The dots indicate words that are unreadable. There is only an attempt to write the address and there is no salutation or end signature

Please forgive this scrawl my head still...felt funny...must write ...you didn't answer my last I felt you must be vexed somewhat. Was it about Bob? He is very good if it is business affairs but does not much otherwise...I hadn't seen much of the girls for some time until Clare got so poorly There are so many now for the... I don't know all their names. But I send things being...now have been sending gift to her for some time. I went out some time back but it is five pounds...so one can't go often especially now one's feet are so bad.

Perhaps you think I spent all the money you so kindly sent me on myself but I kept a share each for Olive and the others and I have sent the West ones girls £60 and clothes and things and the boys something but they do well at work .I don't know a number of the others but will send some more to Olive because she is ill. I must end this letter because I can't write yet...

The closing line of Emilie's final letter is illegible.

Dear Angelique,
In March 2002, Wendy Johnson discovered two letters, written in June
1955, by Mrs Ethel Ellis, Marion's 80 year-old mother, when she was
on a three month, UK tour. The first was dated June 27th 1955 and
among her various, planned excursions, she mentions, "tomorrow we
will go along to Hastings to see Emilie Crane, she is in a nursing home
and may not know me". This is followed by a much longer letter, from
which I quote the relevant paragraphs:-

The George Hotel,
Battle,
Sussex.
June 28th 1955.

Marion Dear,

When I got to the nursing home in Hastings it was to find Emilie had
gone to her niece in London-went last Friday and was to return with
Mrs Newman's son this evening. Mrs Newman was out and this was
all I could elicit from the maid; she said Mrs Newman would be back
in an hour. I went back to the car and we put in that time and returned
to find Mrs Newman at home. She was not keen on saying much about
Emilie but soon I had the whole story. She says E is better physically
but she is very forgetful-she takes a lot of waiting on and Mrs N has to
see Emilie's clothes are on and none forgotten-she is untidy. She
smokes too much for her own good (40 cigs in 2 days). Then people
are after her for money for one thing and another. She gives them
money one week- has to be stopped from doing it over the next-spends
very freely, in fact is terribly extravagant. Her nephew and nieces can
do nothing about it. She hates to see her being done-she talks to her -
she says she is trying to do better.

As I was talking to her in the entry, a doctor went in to see an old lady
of 90. She had been a nurse and had nursed Florence Nightingale. This
90 year-old lady and Emilie are good friends- if either gets bored, they
hunt the other up. Mrs N is also a nurse and has been giving all her
attention to the 90 one-she is now much better. Mrs N is so genuinely
bothered about Emilie, there seems to be nothing to be done but let her
please herself so I left messages for her and came back here.
Love to you honey, England is a wonderful world.
Dearest love to you, Mother.

It was by sheer chance that I came upon a picture and news item in the local newspaper archives, dated 6th October 1951. The photograph shows a very elderly lady smilingly pouring tea under the caption, "Nursed Florence Nightingale". As that was the very same day that I had made my quick tour of Bleaton House, I felt that Emilie was guiding my research!

The article reads:-
"A St Leonards woman who had nursed Florence Nightingale for the last few months before her death, 86 year-old Miss Phoebe Hows, of 7, Warrior Square Gardens, was a guest of the Ritz Cinema on Monday to see the film, "The Lady With A Lamp".
Miss Hows, who was a professional nurse, told an Observer reporter that she was most impressed by the film and although she only knew Miss Nightingale when she was very old, Miss Hows could imagine that Miss Nightingale was just as the film portrayed her.

Miss Hows said she remembered the incident depicted in the film when Sir Douglas Dawson brought the Order of Merit from King Edward VII to the home of Miss Nightingale, but Miss Hows thinks that Miss Nightingale was in bed at the time and not in a chair as the film depicts and that the award was brought to her on a cushion and not in a case. 'I am not quite sure about that", said Miss Hows. "It was a long time ago".

She recalls one night Miss Nightingale asked her where she had received her training. "I replied that I had been to the Elizabeth Fry Institute". A few moments later Miss Nightingale said; "I had the great honour of meeting that lady." Miss Hows added: "She said that to me, while being such a great lady herself". Miss Hows will be 87 next week."

I would say the probability of there being two such women in Hastings and St Leonards and of the appropriate age would be very unlikely and I think that Miss Hows was Emilie's Bleaton House friend.

My own life entered a new phase when, on July 9th 1955, my tiny, golden haired baby girl was born at St Helens Hospital Hastings. In spite of my fears, child birth proved to be a relatively easy affair for me. I recall overhearing the doctor's coarse reference to, "shelling peas". Oh yes? He should try it! She was born just before the convicted murderess, Ruth Ellis was hanged. I read the story in the newspapers whilst in hospital and it seemed particularly dreadful to read of the execution of this pretty, blonde girl, just as I had given birth to such a one.

The next and final piece of documentation of Emilie's life is her death certificate. She had moved from Laton Road to nearby St Helen's Crescent; number eighteen, a registered nursing home, in the name of Mrs M L Glenister. Emilie died on September 11th 1955, of a coronary thrombosis, myocarditis and senile dementia, she was recorded as being 82 years old but she was in fact 84. Emilie's ashes were scattered at Charing Crematorium, 'under the second oak', as the records state. A fitting spot for one of life's stalwarts. So far, I have not been able to find any of her UK relatives.

That week's local newspaper, which recorded Emilie's death in its announcement columns, reported the visit to Hastings of two war heroes; Sir Winston Churchill and Field Marshall Lord Montgomery. How Emilie, had she been able, would have enjoyed this momentous visit. Enclosed as I was in the introspective world of a new baby, I knew nothing of the presence in the town of these two great men. Looking back I can hardly believe how detached I was from outside events. Besides, early in that September I was also taken up with the plans to move from the little flat to our first real home- on The Ridge. The house was only a mile or so from where Emilie had been writing her letters from Lavender Cottage.

We lived in our house on the Ridge for 25 years and I came to know well its particular climate, which Emilie mentioned so often. The long bitter winters and late arriving springs, howling gales in autumn, the glorious sunsets and the fresh, breezy summers, as the town, 500 feet below us, sweltered in spells of humidity. My two other children, another daughter, eighteen months after the first and much later, a son, were born at home, on The Ridge. It was there, over a period of years, I saw my husband succumb to the terrible illness which, in effect, took him away from us long before he died at the age of 53.

1955

His well intentioned but old fashioned idea of a wife's role had kept me from shouldering the normal household responsibilities, so there I was, a widow, aged 44 going on 19, with no idea of household management or finances. During the following years I floundered to find my way, learning fast but making horrendous mistakes of all kinds. Eventually, I found the peace and stability which had eluded me. Through difficult times my children were a source of comfort in so many ways. In May of 1999, they helped me buy, set up and learn to use a computer. Together, they built and I wrote for a web site about Hastings. This was instrumental in bringing me interesting experiences and a new way of life. The Internet became my day-long companion and better still, I had started to fulfil a childhood ambition-to write.

One morning in April 2001, I opened our web site message board and there I read:
Does anyone know if the house Lavender Cottage, The Ridge is still there? A cousin of mine lived there for years. I believe she died in 1955. We have many letters written to my aunt, who sent her parcels during the war and after, when supplies were short. They are an interesting account of that period of history. From Wendy Johnson, Canada.

I owe many thanks to Wendy for allowing me to use Emilie's letters to write this book and also to Emilie herself, for whom I have developed considerable affection and respect. Emilie Ethel Crane enabled me, while retracing the last years of her life, to re-discover my own past, to re-experience in imagination its joys and pleasures and come to terms with its disappointments and sorrows.
With love from Victoria